JavaScript D3
IN 20 MINUTES
(Coffee Break Series)

Kenwright

Copyright © 2021 Kenwright
All rights reserved.

No part of this book may be used or reproduced in any manner whatsoever without written permission of the author except in the case of brief quotations embodied in critical articles and reviews.

BOOK TITLE:
JavaScript D3 (Visualization): in 20 Minutes
ISBN-13: 979-8451313169

The author accepts no responsibility for the accuracy, completeness or quality of the information provided, nor for ensuring that it is up to date. Liability claims against the author relating to material or non-material damages arising from the information provided being used or not being used or from the use of inaccurate and incomplete information are excluded if there was no intentional or gross negligence on the part of the author. The author expressly retains the right to change, add to or delete parts of the book or the whole book without prior notice or to withdraw the information temporarily or permanently.

Revision: 03082021
Author: Kenwright

1	JavaScript D3	1
2	Getting Started	7
3	Core Concepts	13
4	Selections	19
5	Data Joins	31
6	Scalable Vector Graphics	41
7	SVG Transforms	51
8	Transitions	61
9	Animations	65
10	Drawing Charts	71
11	Examples	85

Contents

1 JavaScript D3   **1**
    1.1 Introduction 1
    1.2 What is Data-Visualization? 1
    1.3 What is D3 (D3.js) 2
    1.4 Why do we need D3? 3

2 Getting Started   **7**
    2.1 Installation 7
       2.1.1 D3 Library .8
       2.1.2 Dynamically Loading D3 11
       2.1.3 D3 Editor 11
       2.1.4 Web Browser 12

3 Core Concepts   **13**
    3.1 Introduction 13
       3.1.1 Standards/Key-Terms 13

4 Selections   **19**
    4.1 Introduction 19
       4.1.1 Selection Methods 19
       4.1.2 **select()** method 20
       4.1.3 Adding DOM Elements 23
       4.1.4 Modifying Elements 25
       4.1.5 The classed() method 27
       4.1.6 selectAll() method 28

5 Data Joins   **31**
    5.1 Introduction 31

	5.1.1	What is a Data Join? 31
	5.1.2	How Data Join Works? 32
	5.1.3	Data Join Methods 36
	5.1.4	Data Function 38
	5.1.5	Data Types 39

6 Scalable Vector Graphics — 41

- 6.1 Introduction 41
- 6.2 Features of SVG 41
    - 6.2.1 Minimum Working SVG Example 42
    - 6.2.2 SVG and D3 43
    - 6.2.3 Rectangle Element 44
    - 6.2.4 Circle Element 46
    - 6.2.5 Ellipse Element 47

7 SVG Transforms — 51

- 7.1 Introduction 51
    - 7.1.1 HTML SVG Transform Examples 52
    - 7.1.2 Groups (g) 54
    - 7.1.3 D3 SVG Transforms 55
    - 7.1.4 D3 Transform Library 58

8 Transitions — 61

- 8.1 Introduction 61
    - 8.1.1 transition() method 61
    - 8.1.2 Minimal Example 62

9 Animations — 65

- 9.1 Introduction 65
    - 9.1.1 duration() method 66
    - 9.1.2 Transition Lifecycle 68

10 Drawing Charts — 71

- 10.1 Introduction 71
    - 10.1.1 Bar Chart 72
    - 10.1.2 Circle Chart 75
    - 10.1.3 Pie Chart 79
    - 10.1.4 Donut Chart 82

11 Examples 85
    11.1 Variety of D3 Examples 85

1. JavaScript D3

1.1 Introduction

D3 stands for **Data-Driven Documents** . D3 (also sometimes referred to as D3.js) is an open source JavaScript library for manipulating documents based on **data**. D3 is a **dynamic, interactive** online data visualization **framework**. D3 is an important tool for people who're interested in visualizing data.

1.2 What is Data-Visualization?

Data-visualization is the means of communicating information clearly and efficiently via pictorial or graphical means. These graphical means may include statistical graphics, plots, 3-dimensional renders and more.

Through D3 you'll be able to communicate your insights quickly

> **Give It Some Thought**
>
> **Why are Frameworks Important?** Frameworks provide you with the foundation necessary to build JavaScript applications. This saves you the effort of starting from scratch. Instead you're able to take advantage of a testing code-base to get you up and running quickly. In JavaScript's case, this code-base includes a **collection of pre-written libraries**. These libraries elicit specific functionality for your specific programming needs. In essence, a framework defines a structure for you to use. Technically, everything you can do in D3, you could do in Vanilla JavaScript from the ground-up. But how long would that take?

and effectively. You'll be able to visualize and compare data in novel ways that show patterns and trends. Since D3 is a JavaScript framework developed to run in a web-browser, you'll be able to develop and distribute your data visualizations in websites and mobile applications.

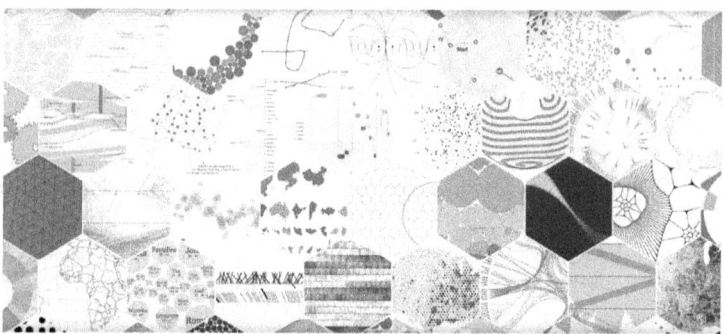

Don't underestimate the power of visualization (especially for data).

1.3 What is D3 (D3.js)

The Data-Driven Documents library known as D3 (or D3.js) is a powerful interactive visualization framework written in

> **Give It Some Thought**
>
> **Why is data visualization important?** The human brain processes information (visually), so using charts or graphs to visualize large amounts of complex data is easier than poring over spreadsheets or reports. Also data visualization can help identify areas that need attention or improvement.

JavaScript for the web. D3 uses the web-browser elements (HTML, CSS, SVG and Canvas) and the **Document Object Model (DOM)** to generate and create content to meet you and your datas desired needs. D3 is an especially valuable tool for **data exploration**, since it gives you complete control over your data's representation (not to mention how you interact with that data).

> **Give It Some Thought**
>
> **What is the Document Object Model (DOM)?** The Document Object Model (DOM) is a programming API for HTML documents. It defines the logical structure of documents and the way a document is accessed and manipulated. The DOM is used as a way of representing many different kinds of information, and much of this would traditionally be seen as data rather than as documents. The Document Object Model (DOM) connects web pages to scripts or programming languages by representing the structure of a document such as the HTML representing a web page in memory.

1.4 Why do we need D3?

D3 is a popular well-established open-source framework that runs in most web-browsers. D3 has a vast assortment of excellent visualization resources, support documentation and examples. However, one of the reasons why D3 is and remains so popular, is owing to its **flexibility**. D3 integrates and works seamlessly with web-based technologies (e.g., HTML, CSS and SVG), including having a large and helpful community of users and developers, which is compounded by its accessibility and straightforwardness to learn.

D3 Features

D3 is able to work with a vast assortment of data types to create both simple and complex visualizations. These visualizations can also be **animated** and **interactive**. Customized user experiences and transition effects. To list some of the key features:

- Easy to user and get started
- Free and open source
- Extremely flexible
- Supports large datasets
- Declarative programming
- Code Reusability
- Wide variety of curve generating functions
- Associate data to elements and groups with the html on the web page

D3 Benefits

Since D3 is an open source project written in JavaScript it does **not** requre any **plugins**. In fact, the library itself is very compact and small.

- Homepage/development: [https://d3js.org/]
- Latest version 2.10.3
- License - free under BSD
- Minified size 116 kb

Few of the core benefits and the rational behind its development are:

- Modular library (download the full library just small pieces depending on your needs)
  - Powerful, eye-catching visualizations (stand out from the crowd)

1.4 Why do we need D3?

- Enables DOM manipulation (controlling web-page)
- Easy to extend/create basic (standard) charts/visual components
- Easy to install

2. Getting Started

2.1 Installation

Getting started with D3 (that is installing and configuring your environment/system to run a D3 program). The essential components you need to get up and running are:

• D3 Library (e.g., either downloading the d3.js directly or referencing it via CDN link)
• Editor (any text editor as long as it support standard unformatted text/UTF8)
• Web-browser (run and test your implementations)

• Web-server (while not totally crucial, for download/streaming data, through to a web-page, this is usually easier using a web-server, due to security constrains with opening/running files locally on a web-page).

You'll learn how to put all the pieces together in this chapter.

2.1.1 D3 Library

You need to include the D3 library (d3.js) in all your HTML webpages in order to use D3 (to create data visualization solutions). There are two main ways of including D3 in your program:

1. Download and include the d3.js library in your project folder

2. Or include a references to the d3.js library from the CDN (**Content Delivery Network**)

Downloading D3

Since D3 is a free and open-source library the source code and distributions are available online at:

- [D3 Webpage: https://d3js.org/](https://d3js.org/)

If you go to the D3 website you can download the latest version of D3 (d3.min.js). As of now, the latest version is **v7.0.0** .

After you've downloaded the latest version of D3, you should

2.1 Installation

> **Give It Some Thought**
>
> 'min' builds - The **min** in the js filename means it is a **minified version** of the javascript file. The script will have every name translated, keeping the same relationships and stuff. This is useful because the file size will be much lower meaning faster downloads and less bandwidth used for the hosting servers

have a 'd3.min.js' file. Create a project folder, which you'll use to run/test your first D3 program. Then make sur eyou copy the 'd3.min.js' file to this folder.

> **Give It Some Thought**
>
> 'd3.min.js' - If you're including your D3 file locally, be sure to include library file in any future project folders you create, so you can access/run the D3 library (if you forget to include the d3 library your program won't run).

For example, create a 'js' folder and include 'd3.min.js' and then you'll include and reference D3 as shown in the HTML example below:

```
<!DOCTYPE html>
<html lang="en">
  <head>
    <script src='./js/d3.min.js'></script>
  </head>
  <body>
    <script>
      // this is where you'll write your D3 code!!
    </script>
  </body>
</html>
```

D3 is a JavaScript library, so all of your code should be written between `<script>` tags. You may also manipulate the existing page configuration (that is the DOM elements), so you want to keep your D3 code inbetween the body tags (i.e., between the opening `<body>` tag and the closing `</body>` tag.

Including D3 Library from CDN

If you prefer not to download the js library to your project folder, instead you can link directly to a version of the d3.min.js online. One such popular reference is the Content Delivery Network (CDN). The CDN offers a collection of servers which host files for users (also take into account geographic location for speed). Taking advantage of this, means you don't need to keep copies of the D3 library, not to mention, it could be faster for users to download the library from the CDN network (versus your hosting).

The D3 library using the CDN URL looks like this:

- [https://cdnjs.cloudflare.com/ajax/libs/d3/7.0.0/d3.min.js]

> **Give It Some Thought**
>
> CDNJS - You can also visit https://cdnjs.com/ website directly and search for hosted versions of files available. For example, you may wish to search and link to a specific version of D3.
>
> Homepage also provides a link to the latest builds of D3 [https://d3js.org/d3.v7.min.js]

An example is given below which uses the CDN link for including D3 in your webpage:

```html
<!DOCTYPE html>
<html lang="en">
  <head>
    <script src='https://cdnjs.cloudflare.com/ajax/libs/d3/7.0.0/
        ↪ d3.min.js'></script>
  </head>
  <body>
    <script>
      // this is where you'll write your D3 code!!
    </script>
  </body>
</html>
```

2.1.2 Dynamically Loading D3

There may be occasions when you want to load D3 dynamically (i.e., you can load the D3 script manually in your code). This is shown in the following listing below, it loads the D3 library using the 'script' element. Remember to check if the script has been loaded. In the example below, the D3 library version is printed to the console window (e.g., ["4.13.0"] for version 4 below, but see what version number you get for library 'd3.v7.min.js').

Listing 2.1: Input

```javascript
var script = document.createElement('script');
script.src = 'https://d3js.org/d3.v4.min.js';
document.head.appendChild(script);

script.onload = function(){
  console.log( d3.version );
}
```

2.1.3 D3 Editor

You need some sort of editor to get started writing your own D3 programs. Luckily, there are lots of great editors available (free and full of powerful features). Some editors go above and beyond basic **text visualization**, but also offer intelligent word prediction (itelisense), auto indentation and error checking. These more complex editors are often referred to as IDEs (Integrated Development Environments). Some examples include:

- Visual Studio Code
- WebStorm
- Eclipse
- Submlime Text

Some IDEs will also support a variety of JavaScript frameworks and offer advanced features. Of course, you don't have to use a complex IDE, you can still always use a simple text editor, such as, Notepad or VI.

2.1.4 Web Browser

D3 runs on all modern browsers (Chrome, Firefox, Edge and so on).

Web-Server

indexweb-server While you can run D3 in a local browser without problems, to access data/resources, you'll want to host your webpage online. This is to prevent you hiting certain restrictions when it comes to loading data for your visualization projects.

As you'll learn, usually you'll store your data seperate from your main D3 program, in files like csv or json formats, that you'll load on-the-fly.

For your web-hosting, any web-server is fine (ISS, Apache, Python, ..).

Running/Viewing your Page

Once you've got your web-server up and running, to view your web-page (i.e., open your HTML in your browser), all you need to do is to navigate to your page URL address. If you're hosting your server **locally**, then you would open your web-browser and type the URL 'http://localhost/' to access and view your page.

3. Core Concepts

3.1 Introduction

D3 is Data-Driven Library written in JavaScript for:

- Dynamically manipulating the Document Object Model (DOM)
- Working with data and shapes
- Providing effective and efficient user interactions
- Enabling smooth transitions between user interfaces (UIs)
- Layering/managing visual elements in linear, hierarchical, network and geographical forms

3.1.1 Standards/Key-Terms

There are a number of standards/definitions that are important when using D3 (as these terms/words are common/heavily used in web-development circles). This includes:

- HyperText Markup Language (HTML)
- Document Object Model (DOM)
- Cascading Style Sheets (CSS)
- Scalable Vector Graphics (SVG)
- JavaScript

If you're already familiar with these concepts, then you may skip ahead, however, to be complete, we'll explain each of them in detail.

HyperText Markup Language (HTML)

As you have have realised by now, HTML is the language used to **structure** the contents of a web-page. HTML is a **text** based language with the extension **.html**.

A minimum (bare-bone) example of what a HTML file looks like:

```html
<!DOCTYPE html>
<html lang='en'>
  <head>
    <meta charset='utf8'>
    <title>Your Title</title>
  </head>
  <body>
    <!-- comment -->
  </body>
</htm>
```

You should notice the essential tags which are common to nearly all web-pages (`html`, `meta`, `title`, `head`, `body`). In addition, you can add comments to html files, which are not displayed on screen, these are between the <- --> tags.

Document Object Model (DOM)

After the web-page is loaded, the structured HTML (tags) are parsed and allow the web-browser to build a hierarchical structure of the page. Every tag in the HTML file is converted to an **element/object** in the DOM (in a parent-child hierarchy). This makes your HTML form a logical structure that is easy to navigate and manage. Once the DOM is formed, you're ready to add, modify or remove any elements on the page using JavaScript (and D3).

Example of a simple DOM given the following HTML:

```
<!DOCTYPE html>
<html lang='en'>
  <head>
    <meta charset='utf8'>
    <title>Your Title</title>
  </head>
  <body>
    <div>
      <h1>Hello Sweet World</h1>
      <p>Would the code taste sweeter in any other language!</p>
    </div>
  </body>
</htm>
```

¿Note, when you write your html, it's usually cleaner and easier to read if you 'indent' the tags based on their 'depth' (i.e., parent-child dependency).

The document object model for the above HTML would be:

```
[Document]
  ->[HTML]
    ->[head]
      ->[title]
        (Your Title)
    ->[body]
      ->[div]
        ->[h1]
          (Hello sw...)
        ->[p]
          (Would the ...)
```

Cascade Style Sheets (CSS)

HTML gives your web-page content and structure (but no **styling**/visual information). This is where CSS comes in. CSS styles makes your web-page more attractive visually (nicer to look at/sexy). CSS is a **Style Sheet Language** and is used to describe the **visual** aspects of your document/page. Each of the elements and objects visual presentation details are defined using CSS (e.g., color, margins, position, and so on).

Scalable Vector Graphics (SVG)

SVG allows you to create bespoke/detailed graphical effects. Importantly, SVG is not a direct image (i.e., doesn't generate 'pixels'). Instead, as the name suggests, it generates 'vector art'. The **scalable** word in SVG means the graphic is able to resize to the necessary dimensions **without distortion**. Nearly all browsers support SVG graphics. SVG is important, as it's a crucial tool for creating powerful data-visualizations using D3.

You create and use SVG graphics as you would any other element. You use the `<svg>` tag to specify a 'region/area' that you'll drawn on (vector lines and shapes). For example:

```
<svg width='500' height='500'></svg>
```

The default measurement of SVG (height/width) is in pixels, so you do not need to specify any units. Now, if you wan tot draw a rectangle in your 'svg' region, you'd type the following:

```
<svg width='400' height='300'>
  <rect x='0' y='0' width='300' height='200'></rect>
</svg>
```

Listing 3.1: Input

```
<svg width='400' height='250'>
  <rect x='0' y='0' width='300' height='200'></rect>
</svg>
```

Figure 3.1: Screen for Listing 3.1

3.1 Introduction

You can draw other shapes in the SVG element area as well (not just rectangles). Range of shapes and drawing styles, including lines, circles, ellipses, text and paths.

Similar to HTML elements, the SVG elements also have styling options. For example, to set the background color using the `fill` keyword inside the `rect` tag. You can even specify the border line color using the `stroke` keyword, as shown below:

Listing 3.2: Input

```
<svg width='400' height='250'>
  <rect x='0' y='0' width='300' height='200' fill='blue'
      ↪ stroke-width='10' stroke='pink'></rect>
</svg>
```

Figure 3.2: Screen for Listing 3.2

JavaScript

JavaScript is a powerful scripting language that you use to execute custom commands to your browser. JavaScript is a `loosly` typed language that interacts with the HTML elements (DOM) and styles.

> **Give It Some Thought**
> A loosely typed language is a programming language that does not require a variable to be defined.

To ensure consistency between browsers, the JavaScript language must conform to a set of standards (**ECMAScript standards**). These standards help ensure core features and functionality work the same for all of your programs (and your D3 library).

4. Selections

4.1 Introduction

A core concept of D3 are **selections**. D3 selection are based on CSS selections. They allow you to select one or more elements on a web-page. Moreover, it allows you to **modify**, **append** or **remove** elements in relation to your dataset(s).

4.1.1 Selection Methods

There aer two main methods for selecting elements, these are:

• **select()** - lets you select **one** DOM element by matching the given CSS selector. If there are more than one element for the given selector, it selects the first one.

• **selectAll()** - lets you select multiple elements by matching the given CSS selector.

4.1.2 select() method

In CSS selectors, you can define and access HTML elements in one of three ways:

- **Tag** identifier of HTML element(e.g., div, h1, span, p, h2, ...)
- **Class Name** of the HTML element
- **ID** of the HTML element.

The D3 select() method selects the HTML method based on the CSS selectors.

Let's look at examples of each.

Selection by Tag

Using the HTML **TAG** name, you can select the HTML elements. The following example, selects the `div` tag elements:

```
d3.select('div');
```

Examples

Selection by Tag Name For this example, you'll create a HTML page with some TAGS (i.e., div elements), then select and modify their content. As you'll notice below, you'll include the D3 script, you add a 'div' tag, then you write your script code at the bottom of the page between the `<script>` tags. The code selects the div, gets the text using `text()`, which you output to the console window.

Listing 4.1: Input

```
<!DOCTYPE html>
<html>
  <head>
```

```html
    <script type='text/javascript' src='https://d3js.org/
        ↪ d3.v7.min.js'></script>
  </head>
  <body>
    <div>
      Hello D3 World! (by tag name)
    </div>

    <script>
      let val = d3.select('div').text();
      console.log( val );
    </script>
  </body>
</html>
```

Listing 4.2: Console for Listing 4.1

```
["\n Hello D3 World! (by tag name)\n "]
```

Hello D3 World! (by tag name)

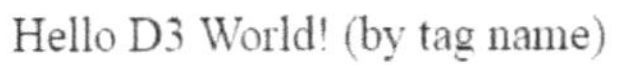

Figure 4.1: Screen for Listing 4.1

Selection by Class name HTML elements styled using CSS classes can be selected using the following syntax:

```
d3.select('<class name>')
```

Let's look at another example below, but this time, you'll select the HTML element using the 'class name'.

Listing 4.3: Input

```html
<!DOCTYPE html>
<html>
  <head>
    <script type='text/javascript' src='https://d3js.org/
        ↪ d3.v7.min.js'></script>
  </head>
  <body>
    <div class='hello'>
      Hello D3 World! (by class name)
    </div>

    <script>
      let val = d3.select('.hello').text();
      console.log( val );
    </script>
  </body>
</html>
```

Listing 4.4: Console for Listing 4.3

```
["\n Hello D3 World! (by class name)\n "]
```

Hello D3 World! (by class name)

Figure 4.2: Screen for Listing 4.3

You should notice when selecting an element using the class name, you need to include the 'dot' before the name (e.g. `.hello` was the class name in the example above).

Selection by ID Typically every element on a HTML should have a **unique ID** assigned to it. You assign a unique ID to an element using the 'id' keyword. You can then retrieve the element using the select() method and the elements ID. You'll use the following syntax:

```
d3.select(#'<id of element>')
```

Let's look at a practical example below that accesses the element using the id (i.e., in the example this id is called 'world').

Listing 4.5: Input

```html
<!DOCTYPE html>
<html>
  <head>
    <script type='text/javascript' src='https://d3js.org/
        ↪ d3.v7.min.js'></script>
  </head>
  <body>
    <div id='world'>
      Hello D3 World! (by id)
    </div>

    <script>
      let val = d3.select('#world').text();
      console.log( val );
    </script>
  </body>
</html>
```

Listing 4.6: Console for Listing 4.5

```
["\n Hello D3 World! (by id)\n "]
```

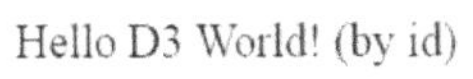

Hello D3 World! (by id)

Figure 4.3: Screen for Listing 4.5

> **Give It Some Thought**
> Note, remember that for class names you should append a dot '.',
> while for tag ids you'd append a hash '#' to the front of the name.
> When using the tag identifier (e.g., div/span/h1), no extra details
> need to be appended.

4.1.3 Adding DOM Elements

Once you can select elements from the DOM, you're then able to extract, add and modify them. For example, as with the `text()` method, which let you access the elements contents, you can also use another method called `append()` to insert/add elements into the existing HTML document.

append() method The `append()` method (as the name might suggest), appends a new element as the **last child** of the current selection. This method can also modify the style of the element, its attributes, properties, HTML and text content.

Let's take a look at a simple example:

Listing 4.7: Input

```html
<!DOCTYPE html>
<html>
  <head>
    <script type='text/javascript' src='https://d3js.org/d3.v7.min.js'></script>
  </head>
  <body>
    <div class='world'>
      Hello D3 World!
    </div>

    <script>
      let val = d3.select('div.world').append('span');
      console.log( val ); // val is the new span
      val.text('test');
    </script>
  </body>
</html>
```

Listing 4.8: Console for Listing 4.7

```
[{"_groups":[[{}]],"_parents":[{}]}]
```

Hello D3 World! test

Figure 4.4: Screen for Listing 4.7

In the example above, you'll notice that you select the `div` tag with the class name `hello`. You then call the `append()` method to add the new element (of type span) as a child. If you were to look at the html, it would be equivalent to:

```
<div class='world'>
  <span>test</span>
</div>
```

The return from the `append()` method is also the new element (i.e., span). Which you can use the `text()` method to retreive or set the text content.

> **Give It Some Thought**
>
> Note you can also **chain** method calls in a single line, known as the **chain syntax** (if prefer this over putting each method and return on seperate lines). For example, instead of storing the newly appended span tag, you could simply call the text method directly on the returned value: `d3.select('div.world').append('span').text('test')`.

For example, on separate lines:

```
let div = d3.select('.hello');
let span = div.append('span');
span.text('test');
```

or using the **chain syntax**, which enables you to perform several actions in a single line of code:

```
d3.select('.hello').append('span').text('test');
```

4.1.4 Modifying Elements

D3 has numerous methods for modifying the DOM. Three important methods that you'll learn about are:

- html()
- attr()
- style()

These methods are especially important for managing the content and style of elements in the DOM.

html() method

The html() method is used to modify the html content of the **selected** or **appended** element. As shown below in the example, you can use the html() method to insert text or add tags (as you would using HTML).

Listing 4.9: Input

```
<!DOCTYPE html>
<html>
  <head>
    <script type='text/javascript' src='https://d3js.org/
        ↪ d3.v7.min.js'></script>
  </head>
  <body>
    <div class='world'>
      Hello D3 World!
    </div>

    <script>
      d3.select('.world').html('Hello <span>from D3</span>' );
    </script>
  </body>
</html>
```

Hello from D3

Figure 4.5: Screen for Listing 4.9

attr() method The attr() method is used to add or update the attributes of an element. In the following example, you'll select an element and add some color information (i.e., styling).

Listing 4.10: Input

```
<!DOCTYPE html>
<html>
  <head>
    <script type='text/javascript' src='https://d3js.org/
      ↪ d3.v7.min.js'></script>
  </head>
  <body>
    <div class='world'>
      Hello D3 World!
    </div>

    <script>
      d3.select('.world').attr('style', 'color: red');
    </script>
  </body>
</html>
```

Hello D3 World!

Figure 4.6: Screen for Listing 4.10

style() method The style() method is used to set the style property of the selected elements.

Listing 4.11: Input

```
<!DOCTYPE html>
<html>
  <head>
    <script type='text/javascript' src='https://d3js.org/
      ↪ d3.v7.min.js'></script>
  </head>
  <body>
    <div class='world'>
      Hello D3 World!
    </div>

    <script>
      d3.select('.world').style('color', 'green');
    </script>
  </body>
</html>
```

Hello D3 World!

Figure 4.7: Screen for Listing 4.11

attr() vs style()

4.1 Introduction

While not always transparent, the `attr()` and `style()` methods may seem very similar? However, the `attr()` sets attributes on the element, while the `style()` method can only modify details within the style area. For example, if you look at the HTML:

```
<text style="fill: red">...
```

vs

```
<text fill="red">...
```

which are both legal in SVG, but using attr when you need style could trip you up if you use it for something else.

4.1.5 The classed() method

The `classed()` method is used to set the **class** attribute of the HTML element. Since an element can have **multiple** classsses (but only a single unique id), the `classed()` method makes this easier to manage.

When setting **class** attributes be sure to use the `classed` method. As the `classed` method knows how to handle one or more class name attributes (that are formatted and arranged to align with the desired specification).

• Add class (**true**) - to add a class to an element you call the **classed()** method with the name of the class to add and the **true** parameter:

```
d3.select('.hello').classed('hot', true);
```

• Remove class (**false**) - to remove a class, you follow the same syntax as the add, but you pass **false** as the second parameter to the **classed()** method.

```
d3.select('.hello').classed('hot', false);
```

• Check class - to check if the class **exists**, just leave off the second parameter and pass the name of the class you're looking for (returns **true** if it exists and **false** if not).

- Toggle class - to **flip** (or toggle) a class to the opposite state - remove it if it exists already (or add it if it does not exist yet), you would do the following:

```
d3.select('.hello').classed('hot', !d3.select('.hello').classed('
    ↪ hot') );
```

or on multiple lines:

```
let hello = d3.select('.hello');
let has = hello.classed('hot');
hello.classed('hot', !has );
```

4.1.6 selectAll() method

The `select()` method was only capable of selecting a **single** element. However, the `selectAll()` method allows you to select **multiple** elements in the HTML document. The `selectAll()` follows the same syntax as the `select()` method, but returns all the elements that meet the critera specified in the input string (e.g., all the elements that have a matching class name, not just the first).

If the `selectAll()` method cannot find any matching elements based on the name criteria you've provided it returns **empty** selection.

Listing 4.12: Input

```
<!DOCTYPE html>
<html>
  <head>
    <script type='text/javascript' src='https://d3js.org/
        ↪ d3.v7.min.js'></script>
  </head>
  <body>
    <div class='world'>
      Hello D3 World!
    </div>

    <script>
      // return 'empty' no elements D3 can't find the
      // elements based on the select criteria

      console.log( d3.select('.wor2ld') ); // typo 'wor2ld'
          ↪ instead of world
      console.log( d3.selectAll('.wor2ld') );

      console.log( d3.selectAll('.wor2ld'));
```

```
      console.log( d3.selectAll('.world' )); // correct spelling
    </script>
  </body>
</html>
```

Listing 4.13: Console for Listing 4.12

```
[{"_groups":[[null]],"_parents":[{}]}]
[{"_groups":[{}],"_parents":[{}]}]
[{"_groups":[{}],"_parents":[{}]}]
[{"_groups":[{"0":{}}],"_parents":[{}]}]
```

Hello D3 World!

Figure 4.8: Screen for Listing 4.12

As with the `select()` method, you can also use `append()`, `html()`, `text()`, `attr()`, `style()` and `classed()` with the `selectAll()` method. The difference is the affected changes will be applied to **all** the selected items (not just a single item).

The following example changes the color of all the elements with the class name 'hot' to red. Notice both the `<h1>` and `<div>` tag style color properties are changed (as they have the class name 'hot' associated with them). Yet the `<span>` tag remains unchanged.

Listing 4.14: Input

```
<!DOCTYPE html>
<html>
  <head>
    <script type='text/javascript' src='https://d3js.org/
        ↪ d3.v7.min.js'></script>
  </head>
  <body>
    <h1 class='hot' >Heading</h1>
    <div class='hot' >
      Once upon a time,
    </div>
    <span> there was </span> ...

    <script>
      d3.selectAll('.hot').style('color', 'red');
    </script>
  </body>
</html>
```

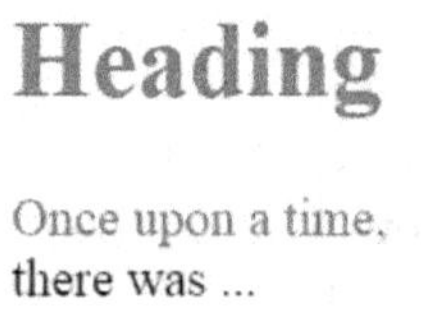

Heading

Once upon a time,
there was ...

Figure 4.9: Screen for Listing 4.14

5. Data Joins

5.1 Introduction

The data join concept is an important topic that works alongside the D3 selection by enabling you to inject, modify and remove elements based on your data sets.

5.1.1 What is a Data Join?

Data join allows you to connect your data with the your HTML elements (i.e., a specific data set value may correspond to an elements graphical appearance). As the data set changes, the corresponding elements can also change (**relationship between the data and elements**). Data join makes it straightforward and easy to manipulate elements in the DOM based on your data set.

5.1.2 How Data Join Works?

Data join works by **mapping** the elements in a document to a given data set. The document then forms a virtual representation based on the given data set. As the data changes so do the elements.

For example, given the following list of numbers:

[10, 20, 30, 40, 50, 60]

The data set has six items and so it can be mapped to six elements. For this example, you'll map the list of elements to a list tag (i.e., **li**).

Listing 5.1: Input

```
<!DOCTYPE html>
<html>
  <head>
    <script type='text/javascript' src='https://d3js.org/
    ↪ d3.v7.min.js'></script>
  </head>
  <body style='height:50pt;'>
    <ul id='list'>
      <li></li>
      <li></li>
    </ul>

    <script>
      let dset = [10,20,30,40,50,60];
      d3.select('#list').selectAll('li').data( dset );
    </script>
  </body>
</html>
```

-
-

Figure 5.1: Screen for Listing 5.1 (Note it should just be empty bullet points outputted to the screen at this stage).

The above example, doesn't show much yet, however, the two **li** elements are now associated with the first two data set values:

5.1 Introduction

- 1. li - 10
- 2. li - 20

You'll now take this further by modifying the methods using **attr()**, **style()**, **text()** for the first two **li** tags.

Listing 5.2: Input

```
<!DOCTYPE html>
<html>
  <head>
    <script type='text/javascript' src='https://d3js.org/
        ↪ d3.v7.min.js'></script>
  </head>
  <body style='height:50pt;'>
    <ul id='list'>
      <li></li>
      <li></li>
    </ul>

    <script>
      let dset = [10,20,30,40,50,60];
      d3.select('#list')
      .selectAll('li')
      .data( dset )
      .text( function(d){ return d; } );
    </script>
  </body>
</html>
```

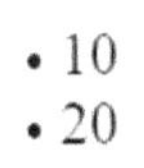

- 10
- 20

Figure 5.2: Screen for Listing 5.2

The `text()` method in the above example is used to get the data value. In the above example, the d represents 10 for the first element and 20 for the second element.

The next six data values can be mapped to any elements. You can use the data join's `enter()` and selector's `append()` method. The `enter()` method gives you access to the remaining data, which is currently not mapped (only the first two data items are). The `append()` method is used to create **new** elements from the corresponding data.

In the following example, you'll create **li** tags for the remaining data values.

Listing 5.3: Input

```
<!DOCTYPE html>
<html>
  <head>
    <script type='text/javascript' src='https://d3js.org/
    ↪ d3.v7.min.js'></script>
  </head>
  <body style='height:80pt;'>
    <ul id='list'>
      <li></li>
      <li></li>
    </ul>

    <script>
    let dset = [10,20,30,40,50,60];
    d3.select('#list')
    .selectAll('li')
    .data( dset )
    .text( function(d){ return d; } )
    .enter()
    .append('li')
    .text( function(d) { return 'dynamically created:' + d; } );
    </script>
  </body>
</html>
```

- 10
- 20
- dynamically created:30
- dynamically created:40
- dynamically created:50
- dynamically created:60

Figure 5.3: Screen for Listing 5.3

Another important data join method worth learning is the `exit()` method. The `exit()` method processes the data items that have been removed dynamically from the data set.

```
d3.selectAll('li')
.data( [10,20] )
.exit()
.remove();
```

This short code sample removes two items from the data set and its **corresponding li** elements using the `exit()` and `remove()` methods.

5.1 Introduction

Listing 5.4: Input

```html
<!DOCTYPE html>
<html>
  <head>
    <script type='text/javascript' src='https://d3js.org/
        d3.v7.min.js'></script>
  </head>
  <body style='height:120pt;'>
    <ul id='list'>
      <li></li>
      <li></li>
    </ul>

    <button onclick='remove();'>Remove</button>

    <script>
      let dset = [10,20,30,40,50,60];
      d3.select('#list')
      .selectAll('li')
      .data( dset )
      .text( function(d){ return 'pre-existing:' + d; } )
      .enter()
      .append('li')
      .text( function(d) { return 'dynamically created:' + d; } );

      function remove() {
        // new data set - 3 items
        dset = [10,20,30];
        d3.selectAll('li')
        .data( [30,30,40] )
        .exit()
        .remove();
      }
    </script>
  </body>
</html>
```

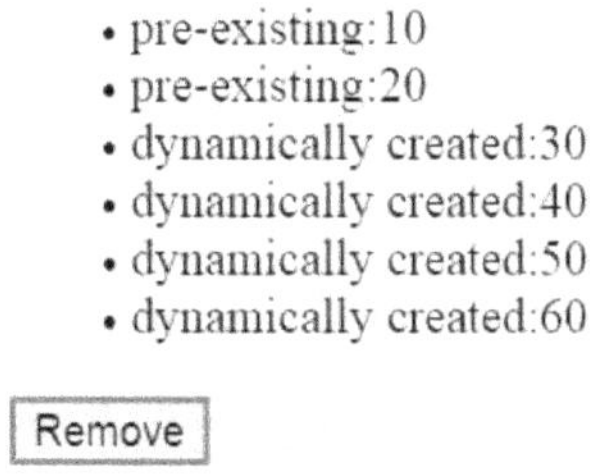

- pre-existing:10
- pre-existing:20
- dynamically created:30
- dynamically created:40
- dynamically created:50
- dynamically created:60

Remove

Figure 5.4: Screen for Listing 5.4

5.1.3 Data Join Methods

The four main methods for data joining are:

- datum()
- data()
- enter()
- exit()

datum() Method

The `datum()` method is used to set values for a **single** element. You use it once for the element you've selected using the selectors. For instance, you can select an existing element (h1 tag) using the `select()` method and then set the data using the `datum()` method. Once the data is set, you can either update/change the text of the selected element or add new elements and assign text using the data set by the `datum()` method.

Listing 5.5: Input

```
<!DOCTYPE html>
<html>
  <head>
    <script type='text/javascript' src='https://d3js.org/
        ↪ d3.v7.min.js'></script>
  </head>
  <body style='height:60pt;'>
    <p>Cats like Mice</p>
    <div>Dogs like Cats</div>

    <script>
    d3.select('p')
    .datum(10)
    .text( function(d){ return 'Existing P data:' + d; } );

    d3.select('div')
    .datum(50)
    .append('p')
    .text( function(d){ return 'New P data:' + d; } );
    </script>
  </body>
</html>
```

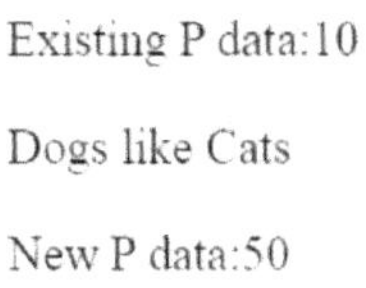

Existing P data:10

Dogs like Cats

New P data:50

Figure 5.5: Screen for Listing 5.5

data() Method

The `data()` method is used to assign a **data set** to a collection of HTML elements. After you've **selected** the element, you use the `data()` method to assign the data. As demonstrated earlier with the `li` tag.

```
d3.selectAll('li')
.data([10,20,30,40]);
```

enter() Method

The `enter()` method outputs the set of **data items for which no graphical element exists**. For instance, in the example where you assigned the data set to an existing list of **li** tags, the data set items that didn't get assigned were retrieved using the `enter()` method.

```
d3.select('#list')
.selectAll('li')
.data([10,20,30,40])
.enter()
.append('li')
.text( function(d){ 'appended:' + d; } );
```

exit() Method

The `exit()` method outputs the set of graphic elements for which no data exists (e.g., either not assigned or has been removed).

```
d3.selectAll('li')
.data([10,20]) // new data set
.exit() // identify the elements with no data
.remove(); // remove these items
```

5.1.4 Data Function

Certain methods, such as, **style()** and **text()** normally take constant input parameters. In the context of **data join**, the methods take **anonymous functions** as a parameter. The anonomous ufnction takes corresponding dadat and the index of the data set assigned using the `data()` method. This anonymous funciton is called for each data value bound to the DOM. For example:

```
.text( function(d,i){
   return d;
});
```

Inside this function, you can apply any logic to manipulate or access the data. These anonymous functions, meaning that there is no name associated with the function. Other than the data(d) and index(i) parameters, you can access the current object using the **this** keyword.

```
.text( function(d,i){
   console.log( d ); // data element
   console.log( i ); // data index
   console.log( this ); // current DOM
   return d;
});
```

Let's look at a working example:

Listing 5.6: Input

```
<!DOCTYPE html>
<html>
  <head>
    <script type='text/javascript' src='https://d3js.org/
    ↪ d3.v7.min.js'></script>
  </head>
  <body style='height:90pt;'>
    <p></p>
    <p></p>
    <p></p>

    <script>
    let mydata = [3,4,5,6,7];
    d3.selectAll('p')
    .data( mydata )
    .text( function(d, i)
    {
        console.log( 'd:', d );
        console.log( 'i:', i );
        console.log( 'this:', this );
        return 'Index:'+i+',Data:'+d+',this:'+this;
```

```
  } );
    </script>
  </body>
</html>
```

Listing 5.7: Console for Listing 5.6

```
["d:",3]
["i:",0]
this:,[object HTMLParagraphElement]
["d:",4]
["i:",1]
this:,[object HTMLParagraphElement]
["d:",5]
["i:",2]
this:,[object HTMLParagraphElement]
```

Index:0,Data:3,this:[object HTMLParagraphElement]

Index:1,Data:4,this:[object HTMLParagraphElement]

Index:2,Data:5,this:[object HTMLParagraphElement]

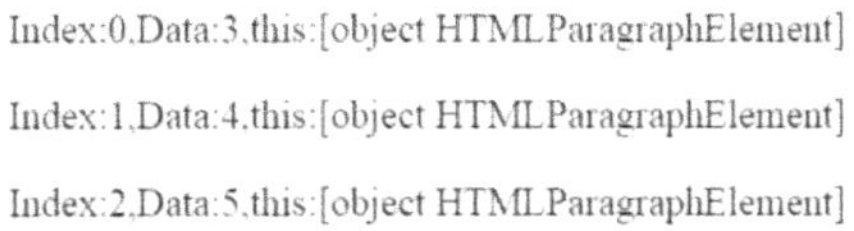

Figure 5.6: Screen for Listing 5.6

In the above example, the parameter **d** gives you your data element, **i** gives you the index of the data, and **this** is a references to the current DOM element. For the above code, **this** is a 'HTMLParagraphElement', since you selected p tags.

5.1.5 Data Types

Just to note, in the simple examples earlier, a basic array of numbers was used, however, you can also use more complicated data structure, for example, array of objects/key-value pairs.

```
let mydata = [ { text:'test', color:'blue', y:'20' },
               { text:'abc' , color:'red', y:'100' } ];
```

Listing 5.8: Input

```
<!DOCTYPE html>
<html>
  <head>
    <script type='text/javascript' src='https://d3js.org/
        ↪ d3.v7.min.js'></script>
  </head>
```

Chapter 5. Data Joins

```
<body style='height:90pt;'>
  <p></p>
  <p></p>

  <script>
  let mydata = [ { text:'test', color:'blue', y:'20' },
                 { text:'abc' , color:'red', y:'100' } ];

  d3.selectAll('p')
  .data( mydata )
  .text( function(d, i)
  {
          this.style['color'] = d.color;
          return d.text;
  } );
  </script>
  </body>
</html>
```

test

abc

Figure 5.7: Screen for Listing 5.8

6. Scalable Vector Graphics

6.1 Introduction

Scalable Vector Graphics ore more commonly referred to as **SVG** is an XML-based **vector** graphics format (compared to pixel-based solutions, vector formats have infinite resolution). Using SVG enables you to take D3 to new levels. SVG provides options to draw different shapes such as lines, rectangles, circles and more. As you might have guessed, D3 fully supports SVG, as it enables you to design more powerful and flexible visualizations.

6.2 Features of SVG

Some of the core features of SVG are:

- SVG has a similar structure to HTML
- SVG is a **vector** based image format that is represented using

'text'
- SVG can be represented as a Document Object Model
- SVG can be included in your HTML document (most modern browsers fully support the SVG format)
- SVG properties can be specified as attributes
- SVG shoudl have absolute positions relative to the origin (0,0)

6.2.1 Minimum Working SVG Example

So you can see how SVG images work, let's add an SVG image to a HTML document.

Step 1 Create an SVG image (container) with a width and height of 300 pixels:

```
<svg width='300' height='300'>
</svg>
```

> **Give It Some Thought**
> Note the default size attributes of the SVG tag are in pixels.

Step 2 Create a line starting at (50,50) and ending at (100,100). Also set the color of the line to 'blue'.

```
<svg width='300' height='300'>
  <line x1='50' y1='50' x2='100' y2='100' style='stroke:rgb
      ↪ (0,0,255);stroke-width:5' />
</svg>
```

The line tag needs to be a child of the SVG container (i.e., you can't just put it anywhere in the DOM). The line tag draws a line from x1,y1 to x2,y2, which are the starting and ending points. To configure the color and line with you need to modify the `style` value. You set the 'stroke' and 'stroke-width' styles.

To reiterate:

- **x1** first x-coordinate point (start)
- **y1** first y-coordinate point (start)
- **x2** second x-coordinate point (end)

6.2 Features of SVG

- **y2** second y-coordinate point (end)
- **stroke** color of the line
- **stroke-width** thickness of the line

Put it all together in a complete HTML example

Listing 6.1: Input

```
<!DOCTYPE html>
<html>
  <head>
    <script type='text/javascript' src='https://d3js.org/
        ↪ d3.v7.min.js'></script>
  </head>
  <body>
    <svg width='300' height='300'>
      <line x1='50' y1='50' x2='100' y2='100' style='stroke:rgb
          ↪ (0,0,255);stroke-width:5' />
    </svg>

    <script>
    </script>
  </body>
</html>
```

Figure 6.1: Screen for Listing 6.1

6.2.2 SVG and D3

You can also create SVG and components using D3, which you'll do now.

Step 1 Create an SVG element and add it to the body of the DOM

```
var svg = d3.select("body") //create Svg element
  .append("svg")
  .attr("height",200 )
  .attr("width", 200);
```

Step 2 Select the SVG container using the `select()` method and inject the SVG element using the `append()` method. Add attributes and stules using the `attr()` and `style()` methods.

```
d3.select('svg')
.append('line')
.attr('x1', 30)
.attr('y1', 30)
.attr('x2', 100)
.attr('y2', 100)
.style('stroke', 'rgb(0,255,0)' )
.style('stroke-width', '3' );
```

Let's put it all together for a fully working example

Listing 6.2: Input

```
<!DOCTYPE html>
<html>
  <head>
    <script type='text/javascript' src='https://d3js.org/
        ↪ d3.v7.min.js'></script>
  </head>
  <body>
    <script>
    var svg = d3.select("body") //create svg element
      .append("svg")
      .attr("height",200 )
      .attr("width", 200);

    d3.select('svg')
    .append('line')
    .attr('x1', 30)
    .attr('y1', 30)
    .attr('x2', 100)
    .attr('y2', 100)
    .style('stroke', 'rgb(0,255,0)' )
    .style('stroke-width', '3' );
    </script>
  </body>
</html>
```

6.2.3 Rectangle Element

The `<rect>` tag as shown below:

6.2 Features of SVG

Figure 6.2: Screen for Listing 6.2

```
<rect x='10' y='10' width='30' height='50'></rect>
```

where the attributes are:

- **x** x-coordinate of the top-left corner of the rectangle
- **y** y-coordinate of the top-left corner of the rectangle
- **width** size of the rectangle along the x-axis
- **height** size of the rectangle along the y-axis

Listing 6.3: Input

```
<!DOCTYPE html>
<html>
  <head>
    <script type='text/javascript' src='https://d3js.org/
      ↪ d3.v7.min.js'></script>
  </head>
  <body>
    <script>
    var svg = d3.select("body") //create svg element
      .append("svg")
      .attr("height",200 )
      .attr("width", 200);

    d3.select('svg')
    .append('rect')
    .attr('x', 30)
    .attr('y', 30)
    .attr('width', 100)
    .attr('height', 50)
    .attr('fill', 'rgb(0,0,255)' );
    </script>
  </body>
</html>
```

Figure 6.3: Screen for Listing 6.3

6.2.4 Circle Element

A circle is drawn using the `<circle>` tag. For example, you would use it as follows:

```
<circle cx='50' cy='50' r='20' />
```

The attributes of the circle tag are:

- **cx** x-coordinate of the centre of the circle
- **cy** y-coordinate of the centre of the circle
- **r** radius of the circle

A simple example is given below:

Listing 6.4: Input

```
<!DOCTYPE html>
<html>
  <head>
    <script type='text/javascript' src='https://d3js.org/
        ↪ d3.v7.min.js'></script>
  </head>
  <body>
    <script>
    var svg = d3.select("body") //create svg element
      .append("svg")
      .attr("height",200 )
      .attr("width", 200);

    d3.select('svg')
     .append('circle')
     .attr('cx', 100)
     .attr('cy', 30)
     .attr('r', 20)
     .attr('fill', 'rgb(255,0,0)' );
    </script>
  </body>
</html>
```

Figure 6.4: Screen for Listing 6.4

6.2.5 Ellipse Element

The ellipse element as you might have guessed is represented by the `<ellipse>` tag and is used as follows:

```
<ellipse cx='100' cy='20' rx='30' ry='50' />
```

The attributes of the ellipse element are:

- **cx** x-coordinates for the centre position
- **cy** y-coordinates for the centre position
- **rx** radius of the circle along the x-direction
- **ry** radius of the circle along the y-direction

A simple example of the ellipse is given below:

Listing 6.5: Input

```
<!DOCTYPE html>
<html>
  <head>
    <script type='text/javascript' src='https://d3js.org/
        ↪ d3.v7.min.js'></script>
  </head>
  <body>
    <script>
    var svg = d3.select("body") //create svg element
      .append("svg")
      .attr("height",200 )
      .attr("width", 200);

    d3.select('svg')
    .append('ellipse')
    .attr('cx', 100)
    .attr('cy', 30)
    .attr('rx', 70)
    .attr('ry', 20)
    .attr('fill', 'rgb(255,0,255)' );
```

Figure 6.5: Screen for Listing 6.5

¿ Note, if the position of the drawn element is outside of the boundaries of the containing SVG, it will be 'clipped' (i.e., you won't see the parts of the element that leave the SVG edges).

Listing 6.6: Input

```
<!DOCTYPE html>
<html>
  <head>
    <script type='text/javascript' src='https://d3js.org/
        ↪ d3.v7.min.js'></script>
  </head>
  <body>
    <script>
    var svg = d3.select("body") //create svg element
       .append("svg")
       .attr("height",200 )
       .attr("width", 200);

    // randomly put circles
    for (let i=0; i<10; i++)
    {
        svg.append('circle')
        .attr('cx', Math.random()*250)
        .attr('cy', Math.random()*250)
        .attr('r', 10 + Math.random()*50)
        .attr('fill', 'rgb('+Math.random()*255+','
                            +Math.random()*255+','
                            +Math.random()*255+')' );
    }// end for i
    </script>
  </body>
</html>
```

6.2 Features of SVG

Figure 6.6: Screen for Listing 6.6

7. SVG Transforms

7.1 Introduction

The ability to transform SVG graphics enable you to manipulate elements on a higher level (such as scaling, rotating, skewing and translating).

SVG transforms are set through the **transform** attribute. The various transform options available include:

• **Rotation** - takes **three** options which refer to the position of rotation (cx and cy) and the angle. If cx and cy are not specified the position of rotation is taken to be the origin of the shape (that is the centre).

```
transform: rotate(60);
```

• **Translation** - takes two options the translation along the x and y-axis. The the options are referred to as **tx** and **ty**.

```
transform: translate(20, 50);
```

- **Scale** - takes to options for the scaling along the x and y-axis. The options are **sx** and **sy**.

- **Skew** - skew is made of seperate **SkewX** and **SkewY**. The skew option is a single number which refers to the **skew-angle**.

```
transform: skewx(10);
```

> **Give It Some Thought**
>
> Importantly, the different transforms can be combined to form more complex transformations. Also the order the transforms are conncatenated matters (e.g., translation then rotation is not the same as rotation then translation).

7.1.1 HTML SVG Transform Examples

Rotation

Create a simple SVG rectangle and rotate it about 20 degrees.

Listing 7.1: Input

```
<!DOCTYPE html>
<html>
  <head>
    <script type='text/javascript' src='https://d3js.org/
       ↪ d3.v7.min.js'></script>
  </head>
  <body style='height:50pt;'>
    <svg width='100' height='100'>
      <rect x='60' y='20' width='40' height='10' fill='blue'
          transform='rotate(20)'>
      </rect>
    </svg>

    <script>;
    </script>
  </body>
</html>
```

7.1 Introduction

Figure 7.1: Screen for Listing 7.1

Translation

Create a simple SVG rectangle and translate it by 20 pixels along the x axis and 10 pixels along the y axis.

¿ Note if you translate the shape too far (e.g., translate by 100 along the x-axis), it will leave the SVG container region and be clipped (i.e., you won't see the rectangle)

Listing 7.2: Input

```
<!DOCTYPE html>
<html>
  <head>
    <script type='text/javascript' src='https://d3js.org/
        ↪ d3.v7.min.js'></script>
  </head>
  <body style='height:50pt;'>
    <svg width='100' height='100'>
      <rect x='60' y='20' width='40' height='10' fill='blue'
          transform='translate(20,10)'>
      </rect>
    </svg>

    <script>;
    </script>
  </body>
</html>
```

Figure 7.2: Screen for Listing 7.2

Scale

Create a simple SVG rectangle and scale it along the x and y axis.

Listing 7.3: Input

```
<!DOCTYPE html>
<html>
  <head>
    <script type='text/javascript' src='https://d3js.org/
        ↪ d3.v7.min.js'></script>
  </head>
  <body style='height:100pt;'>
    <svg width='100' height='100'>
      <rect x='60' y='20' width='40' height='10' fill='blue'
          transform='scale(1,3)'>
      </rect>
    </svg>

    <script>;
    </script>
  </body>
</html>
```

Figure 7.3: Screen for Listing 7.3

7.1.2 Groups (g)

SVG elements can be grouped together using the `<g>` tag. They essentially become a single shape that can be manipulated as one object. So instead of manipulating lots of individual SVG elements, a single group can be manipulated.

```
<g>
  <rect x='60' y='20' width='40' height='10' fill='blue' ></rect>
  <rect x='160' y='10' width='20' height='10' fill='green'></rect>
</g>
```

7.1 Introduction

You're able to apply transforms to groups and the transforms are applied to all of the contained elements.

Listing 7.4: Input

```
<!DOCTYPE html>
<html>
  <head>
    <script type='text/javascript' src='https://d3js.org/
        ↪ d3.v7.min.js'></script>
  </head>
  <body style='height:100pt;'>
    <svg width='100' height='100'>
      <g transform='scale(1,1)'> <!-- original group -->
        <rect x='60' y='20' width='40' height='10' fill='blue'></
            ↪ rect>
        <circle cx='10' cy='10' r='10' fill='red' />
      </g>

      <g transform='scale(1,3)'> <!-- create copy but transform
          ↪ the group -->
        <rect x='60' y='20' width='40' height='10' fill='blue'></
            ↪ rect>
        <circle cx='10' cy='10' r='10' fill='red' />
      </g>

    </svg>

    <script>;
    </script>
  </body>
</html>
```

Figure 7.4: Screen for Listing 7.4

7.1.3 D3 SVG Transforms

To apply a transform to one or more SVG elements with D3, you simply select the items (for example, using their tag name or ids). You then set their transform attribute.

Chapter 7. SVG Transforms

Listing 7.5: Input

```
<!DOCTYPE html>
<html>
  <head>
    <script type='text/javascript' src='https://d3js.org/
      ↪ d3.v7.min.js'></script>
  </head>
  <body style='height:100pt;'>
    <svg width='200' height='200'>
    </svg>

    <script>
      d3.select('svg')
      .append('rect')
      .attr('x', 30)
      .attr('y', 20)
      .attr('width', 100)
      .attr('height', 50)
      .attr('fill', 'green')
      .attr('transform', 'rotate(10)');
    </script>
  </body>
</html>
```

Figure 7.5: Screen for Listing 7.5

Listing 7.6: Input

```
<!DOCTYPE html>
<html>
  <head>
    <script type='text/javascript' src='https://d3js.org/
      ↪ d3.v7.min.js'></script>
  </head>
  <body style='height:100pt;'>

    <script>
      d3.select('body')
      .append('svg')
      .attr('width', 300)
      .attr('height', 300)
      .append('rect')
```

7.1 Introduction

```
    .attr('x', 30)
    .attr('y', 20)
    .attr('width', 100)
    .attr('height', 50)
    .attr('fill', 'green')
    .attr('transform', 'rotate(10)');
    </script>
  </body>
</html>
```

Figure 7.6: Screen for Listing 7.6

Listing 7.7: Input

```
<!DOCTYPE html>
<html>
  <head>
    <script type='text/javascript' src='https://d3js.org/
        ↪ d3.v7.min.js'></script>
  </head>
  <body style='height:100pt;'>

    <script>
      let svg = d3.select('body')
      .append('svg')
      .attr('width', 300)
      .attr('height', 300);

      let group = svg
      .append('g')
      .attr('transform', 'translate(30,50) rotate(20)'); //
          ↪ truncate transforms

      group
      .append('rect')
      .attr('x', 30)
      .attr('y', 20)
      .attr('width', 100)
      .attr('height', 50)
      .attr('fill', 'green');

      group
      .append('circle')
      .attr('cx', 5)
      .attr('cy', 5)
      .attr('r', 30)
```

```
    .attr('fill', 'blue');
    </script>
  </body>
</html>
```

Figure 7.7: Screen for Listing 7.7

7.1.4 D3 Transform Library

Due to the modular nature of D3, it also provides a seperate library to manage transform attributes. The D3 transform library has methods for all types of transformations. Some of the methods include **transform()**, **translate()**, **scale()** and **rotate()**.

To use the D3 transform library you need to include the **d3-transform** JavaScript library.

Listing 7.8: Input

```
<!DOCTYPE html>
<html>
  <head>
    <script type='text/javascript' src='https://d3js.org/
        ↪ d3.v7.min.js'></script>

    <script type='text/javascript' src='https://
        ↪ cdnjs.cloudflare.com/ajax/libs/d3-transform/1.0.4/
        ↪ d3-transform.min.js'></script>
  </head>
  <body style='height:100pt;'>

    <script>
      let svg = d3.select('body')
        .append('svg')
        .attr('width', 300)
        .attr('height', 300);
```

7.1 Introduction

```
    let d3t = d3Transform()
    .translate([20,10])
    .scale([0.5,1])
    .rotate(10);

    svg.append('rect')
    .attr('x', 30)
    .attr('y', 20)
    .attr('width', 100)
    .attr('height', 50)
    .attr('fill', 'pink')
    .attr('transform', d3t );
  </script>
 </body>
</html>
```

Figure 7.8: Screen for Listing 7.8

To use the d3-transform you:

1 include the JavaScript module 'd3-transform.js' (or minimized version 'd3-transform.min.js')
2 you construct a transform using the **d3Transform()** method (chain individual transforms onto the end)
3 you apply the transform to the SVG by attaching the result from the d3Transform to the graphical element

8. Transitions

8.1 Introduction

The process of changing from one state to another is managed through **transitions**. Due to the importance of smooth clean transitions when presenting your visualizations, D3 has a specific method for managing this called **transition()**.

8.1.1 transition() method

The **transition()** method is available for **all selectors**. In addition to the selectors, the transition method also supports most of the selection methods, such as, style() and attr().

When you call the **transition()** method, you need to be sure that you've setup (called) the **append()** and **data()** methods first. In addition to the **transition()** method, there are a number of control methods, such as **duration()** and **ease()**.

> **Give It Some Thought**
>
> Note the **transition()** method does not support the **append()** or **data()** method (i.e., it cannot impact these methods by transitioning their change). For example, when you change the data, this should happen immediately, and not gradually over time.

Look at the following example, to see how simple it's to integrate transitions into your D3 code:

```
d3.select('body')
.transition()
.style('background-color', 'lightgreen');
```

A transition can be directly created using the `d3.transition()` method followed by the selectors, as follows:

```
let t = d3.transition
.duration(3000);

d3.select('body')
.transition(t)
.style('background-color', 'lightgreen');
```

8.1.2 Minimal Example

Let's create a simple example to see how **transitions** work in a complete implementation.

Listing 8.1: Input

```html
<!DOCTYPE html>
<html>
  <head>
    <script type='text/javascript' src='https://d3js.org/d3.v7.min.js'></script>
  </head>
  <body style='height:50pt;'>
    <h1>Transitions are Amazing</h1>

    <script>
      d3.select('body')
      .transition()
      .style('background-color', 'lightgreen');
    </script>
  </body>
</html>
```

8.1 Introduction

Listing 8.2: Console for Listing 8.1

Transitions are Amazing

Figure 8.1: Screen for Listing 8.1

In the above example, you select the 'body' element and then start transitioning by calling the **transition()** method. You then instruct the transition to change the **background-color** from the current color to **lightgreen**.

When you run (or refresh the example), you should see the background screen color change (gradually) to lightgreen.

You could take the concept further, as shown below, by truncating transitions, so the background color will transition between different colors before stopping. In the example below, the background will change from the current color to lightgreen, to yellow and finally white.

Listing 8.3: Input

```
<!DOCTYPE html>
<html>
  <head>
    <script type='text/javascript' src='https://d3js.org/
       ↪ d3.v7.min.js'></script>
  </head>
  <body style='height:50pt;'>
    <h1>Transitions are Amazing</h1>

    <script>
      d3.select('body')
      .transition()
      .style('background-color', 'lightgreen')
      .transition()
      .style('background-color', 'yellow')
      .transition()
      .style('background-color', 'white');
    </script>
  </body>
</html>
```

duration(), ease() and delay() methods The duration() and ease() methods give you an extra aspect of control, if you want the transitions to be slow or fast (linear or non-linear).

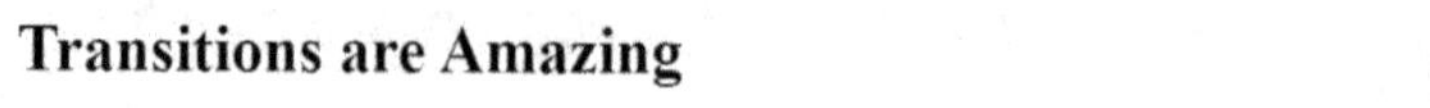

Transitions are Amazing

Figure 8.2: Screen for Listing 8.3

Listing 8.4: Input

```
<!DOCTYPE html>
<html>
 <head>
   <script type='text/javascript' src='https://d3js.org/
       ↪ d3.v7.min.js'></script>
 </head>
 <body style='height:50pt;'>
   <h1>Transitions are Amazing</h1>

   <script>
     d3.select('body')
     .transition()
       .delay(1000) // wait 1 second before starting transition
       .duration(4000) // take 4 seconds the transition
       .ease(d3.easeCubicIn) // transition type
     .style('background-color', 'lightblue');
   </script>
 </body>
</html>
```

Transitions are Amazing

Figure 8.3: Screen for Listing 8.4

9. Animations

9.1 Introduction

Animations bring your data to life. Extending **transitions** D3 is able to create animation effects. In D3 animations are limited to a form of **Key Frame Animation** sequence (i.e., two keys - a start key and an end key). The starting point of the animation is usually taken to be the **current** state (of the DOM elements/attributes/styles). Animation transitions in D3 are elegant and easy to setup (and control).

In the example below, the background color changes from the initial 'blue' to the final 'yellow' color.

Listing 9.1: Input

```
<!DOCTYPE html>
<html>
  <head>
    <script type='text/javascript' src='https://d3js.org/
        ↪ d3.v7.min.js'></script>
  </head>
  <body style='height:50pt;'>
```

```
    <h1>Transitions to Animations</h1>

    <script>
      d3.select('body')
      .style('background-color', 'blue')
      .transition()
      .style('background-color', 'yellow');
    </script>
  </body>
</html>
```

Transitions to Animations

Figure 9.1: Screen for Listing 9.1

9.1.1 duration() method

The **duration()** method transitions to change smoothly over a **specified** duration of time (rather than instantaneously). If you want the transition to take 4 seconds, then you'd set the transition duration as follow:

Listing 9.2: Input

```
<!DOCTYPE html>
<html>
  <head>
    <script type='text/javascript' src='https://d3js.org/
        ↪ d3.v7.min.js'></script>
  </head>
  <body style='height:50pt;'>
    <h1>Transitions to Animations</h1>

    <script>
      d3.selectAll('h1')
      .transition()
      .style('color', 'green')
      .duration(4000);
    </script>
  </body>
</html>
```

In the above example, the **h1** heading text changes color gradually over 4 seconds (default black to green). Also in addition to defining the color using the word, you can also use the 'rgb' define:

9.1 Introduction

Transitions to Animations

Figure 9.2: Screen for Listing 9.2

```
d3.selectAll('h1')
    .transition()
    .style('color', 'rgb(0,255,0)') // use 'rgb' for exact color
        ↪ instead of names like 'green'
    .duration(4000);
```

In the following example, you'll transition the **font-size**, the **color** and the **position** of the **h1** text.

Listing 9.3: Input

```
<!DOCTYPE html>
<html>
  <head>
    <script type='text/javascript' src='https://d3js.org/
        ↪ d3.v7.min.js'></script>
  </head>
  <body style='height:50pt;'>
    <h1>Transitions to Animations</h1>

    <script>
      d3.selectAll('h1')
      .transition()
      .style('font-size', '28pt')
      .style('color', 'pink')
      .style('transform', 'translate(100pt,0)')
      .duration(4000);
    </script>
  </body>
</html>
```

Transitions to Animations

Figure 9.3: Screen for Listing 9.3

D3 takes care of all the interpolation details for you in advance. You just need to specify the desired transition, duration and which parameters to change and everything else is handled for you.

delay() method As you may have guessed from the name, the **delay()** method allows you to add a pause before your transition starts. The **delay()** parameter is the number of milliseconds (1000ms == 1s).

9.1.2 Transition Lifecycle

The D3 transition has a **four-phase** lifecycle:

1. The transition is schedules
2. The transition starts
3. The transition runs
4. The transition ends

Let's review each of these in detail.

The Transition is Scheduled

A **transition** is scheduled when it's created. When we call **selection** and **transition**, you're scheduling a transition. This is also when you call **attr()** and **style()** transition methods to define the end key frame values.

The Transition Start

The transition starts based on the delay, which is specified when the transition is scheduled. If you don't specify a delay, the transition starts as soon as possible (typically after a few milliseconds).

If you specify a delay, the starting value should be set to when you want the transition to start.

```
d3.select('body')
.transition()
.delay(200) // wait 0.2 seconds before starting transition
.on('start', function(){ // callback when transition starts
   d3.select(this).style('color', 'blue')'
   })
.style('color', 'red');
```

The Transitions Runs

When the transition runs, it's repeatedly invoked with values of the transition ranging from **0** to **1**. Also the **delay** and **duration** have easing control timing details. Easing distorts time to create a more asthetically desired result, such as, **slow-in** and **slow-out**. Some easing functions may temporarily give values of **t** greater than **1** or less than **0**.

The Transition Ends

The transition end time value is always exactly **1**. The transition ends based on the sum of its delay and duration. When a transition ends, the **'end'** event is dispatched.

Listing 9.4: Input

```
<!DOCTYPE html>
<html>
  <head>
    <script type='text/javascript' src='https://d3js.org/
        ↪ d3.v7.min.js'></script>
  </head>
  <body style='height:50pt;'>
    <h1>Transitions to Animations</h1>

    <script>
      d3.selectAll('h1')
      .transition()
      .duration(4000)
      .delay(100)
      .on('start', function(){ console.log('transition started....'
          ↪ ); } )
      .style('color', 'pink')
      .style('font-size', '28pt')
      .on('end' , function(){ console.log('transition ended...'); }
          ↪ );

    </script>
  </body>
</html>
```

Listing 9.5: Console for Listing 9.4

```
["transition started...."]
["transition ended..."]
```

Using the **on()** method you can connect event callbacks to let

Transitions to Animations

Figure 9.4: Screen for Listing 9.4

you know when transitions have started or ended (you can also add in extra selects/transitions inside these callbacks to build up a complex set of animations).

> **Give It Some Thought**
>
> Note, take care with D3 version numbers, transition event callbacks was added in D3 version 3.0; older versions of D3 dispatched the start event after constructing tweens (interpolation between two keyframes).
>
> ```
> // d3 v5
> d3.select("#myid").transition().style("opacity","0").on("end"
>     ↪ , myCallback);}\end{quote}
>
> // old way
> d3.select("#myid").transition().style("opacity","0").each("
>     ↪ end", myCallback);
> ```

10. Drawing Charts

10.1 Introduction

One of the oldest ways of visualizing data is through **charts**. Obviously, D3 supports a variety of chart drawing solutions, for example

- Bar Chart
- Pie Chart
- Circle Chart
- Donut Chart
- Line Chart
- Bubble Chart

Let's look at the some of the main chart types and how to create them using D3.

10.1.1 Bar Chart

You're now going to create a bar chart using SVG parts of D3. For this example, you can use the **rect element** for the bars and the **text element** to display details about the data (i.e., axis information and what the bars mean).

Step 1 Adding style in the rect element - add the following style to the rect element

```
svg rect {
  fill: gray;
}
```

Step 2 Add styles in text element - add the following CSS class to apply styles to text values. Add this style to SVG text element.

```
svg text {
  fill: yellow;
  font: 12px san-serif;
  text-anchor: end;
}
```

The CSS **fill** is used to apply colors. Text-anchor is used to position the text towards the right end of the bars.

Step 3 Define the variables - add the variables to the script

```
<script>
let data = [10,5,12,15];
let width = 300;
let scaleFactor = 20;
let barHeight = 30;
</script>
```

- width - width of the SVG

- scaleFactor - scaled to a pixel value that is visible on screen

- barHeight - This is the static height of the horizontal bars

Step 4 Append SVG elements - you append SVG elements in D3 using the following code:

```
let graph = d3.select('body')
.append('svg')
.attr('width', width)
.attr('height', barHeight*data.length );
```

10.1 Introduction

You first select the document body, then you create a new SVG and append it to the body. You then build your bar graph inside the SVG element. You then set the width and height of the SVG. The height is calculated using the bar height times the number of data values.

You have to take the bar height as 30 and the data array is of size 4. Then the height is calculated as `barHeight*data.length` which is 120px.

Step 5 Apply transformation - You apply the transformation to the bar using the following:

```
let bar = graph.selectAll('g')
.data(data)
.enter()
.append('g')
.attr('transform', function(d,i){
   return 'translate(0, '+i*barHeight+')';
});
```

Above, each bar corresponds to an element. There for youc reate a group of elements. Each of your group elemetns needs to be positioned below the other to build a horizontal bar chart. The transformation formula is index multiplied by the bar height.

Step 6 Append rect element to the bar - in the previous step you appended the group elements. Now you add the rect elements to the bar using the following:

```
bar.append('rect')
.attr('width', function(d){
   return d * scaleFactor;
})
.attr('height', barHeight-1);
```

Step 7 Display data - this is the last step, and lets you display the data on each bar using the following:

```
bar.append('text')
.attr('x', function(d){
  return (d*scaleFactor); } )
.attr('y', barHeight/2)
.attr('dy', '.35em')
.text( function(d) { return d; } );
```

In the above, the width is defined as (data value multiplied by the scale factor). Text elements do not support padding or margin.

For this reason, you need to dive it a 'dy' offset. This is used to align the text vertically.

Step 8 Complete working example - the following brings together all of the steps.

Listing 10.1: Input

```
<!DOCTYPE html>
<html>
  <head>
    <script type='text/javascript' src='https://d3js.org/
    ↪ d3.v7.min.js'></script>

    <style>
      svg rect {
        fill: gray;
      }
      svg text {
        fill : yellow;
        font: 12px sans-serif;
        text-anchor: end;
      }
    </style>
  </head>
  <body style='height:100pt;'>

  <script>
    let data = [10,5,15,4];
    let width = 300;
    let scaleFactor = 20;
    let barHeight = 30;

    let graph = d3.select('body')
    .append('svg')
    .attr('width', width)
    .attr('height', barHeight*data.length);

    let bar = graph.selectAll('g')
    .data(data)
    .enter()
    .append('g')
    .attr('transform', function(d,i){
      return 'translate(0, '+i*barHeight+')';
    });

    bar.append('rect')
    .attr('width', function(d) {
      return d*scaleFactor;
    })
    .attr('height', barHeight-1);

    bar.append('text')
    .attr('x', function(d){
        return (d*scaleFactor);
    })
    .attr('y', barHeight/2)
```

10.1 Introduction

```
    .attr('dy', '.35em')
    .text( function(d){ return d; } );

  </script>
  </body>
</html>
```

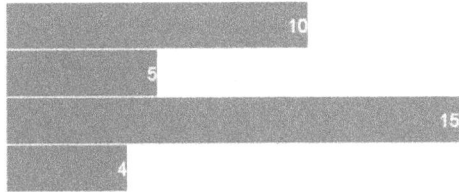

Figure 10.1: Screen for Listing 10.1

10.1.2 Circle Chart

A circle chart is a circular statistical graphic, which is divided into slices to illustrate a numerical proportion.

You'll now learn how to draw a circle chart using D3.

Step 1 Define your variables - you define the variables for your chart in the script:

```
<script>
  let width = 400
  let height = 400;
  let data = [10, 30, 40];
  let colors = ['red', 'green', 'blue'];
</script>
```

- width - width of the SVG
- height - height of the SVG
- data - array of data elements
- colors - colors you'll apply to the circle elements

Step 2 Append SVG elements - you'll now append the SVG elements with D3 using the following

```
let svg = d3.select('body')
.append('svg')
```

```
.attr('width', width)
.attr('height', height);
```

Step 3 Apply transformation - you'll apply the transformation to the SVG using the following

```
let g = svg.selectAll('g')
.data(data)
.enter()
.append('g')
.attr( 'transform', function(d,i) {
   return 'translate(0,0)';
});
```

- `let g = svg.selectAll('g')` - group of elements to hold all the circles
- `.data(data)` - binds your data array to the group elements
- `.enter()` - creates placeholders for your group elements
- `append('g')` appends group elements to your page

```
.attr('transform', function(d,i){
  return( 'translate(0,0)';
})
```

The 'translate' is used to position your elements iwth respect to
  ↪ the origin.

Step 4 Append circle elements - you append the circle elements to the group using the following

```
g.append('circle')
```

You add attributes to the group using the following

```
.attr('cx', function(d,i){
  return i*75 + 50;
})
```

You use the x-coorcinate of the centre of each circle. You multiply the index of the circle with 75 and add some padding (50) between the circles.

Next, you set the y-coordinates of the centre of each circle. This is used to uniform all the circles.

```
.attr('cy', function(d,i){
  return 75;
})
```

10.1 Introduction

You then set the radius of each circle, as given below

```
.attr( 'r', function(d) {
  return d*1.5;
})
```

The radius is multiplied with the data value along with a constant '1.5' to increase the circles size. Finally you use 'fill' to color each circle, as follows

```
.attr('fill', function(d,i){
  return colors[i];
}
```

Step 5 Display data - this is the last step. You display the data on each cirle using the following

```
g.append('text')
.attr('x', function(d,i){
   return ( i*75+25 );
})
.attr('y', 80)
.attr('stroke', 'teal')
.attr('font-size', '10px')
.attr('font-family', 'sans-serif')
.text( function(d) { return d; } );
```

Step 6 Working example - putting all the steps together into a complete example

Listing 10.2: Input

```
<!DOCTYPE html>
<html>
  <head>
    <script type='text/javascript' src='https://d3js.org/
        ↪ d3.v7.min.js'></script>
  </head>
  <body style='height:100pt;'>

  <script>
  let width = 400
  let height = 400;
  let data = [10, 30, 40];
  let colors = ['red', 'green', 'blue'];

  let svg = d3.select('body')
  .append('svg')
  .attr('width', width)
  .attr('height', height);

  let g = svg.selectAll('g')
  .data(data)
  .enter()
```

```
  .append('g')
  .attr( 'transform', function(d,i) {
     return 'translate(0,0)';
  });

  g.append('circle')
  .attr('cx', function(d,i){
    return i*75 + 50;
  })
  .attr('cy', function(d,i){
    return 75;
  })
  .attr( 'r', function(d) {
    return d*1.5;
  })
  .attr('fill', function(d,i){
    return colors[i];
  });

  g.append('text')
  .attr('x', function(d,i){
     return ( i*75+25 );
  })
  .attr('y', 80)
  .attr('stroke', 'teal')
  .attr('font-size', '10px')
  .attr('font-family', 'sans-serif')
  .text( function(d) { return d; } );

  </script>
  </body>
</html>
```

Figure 10.2: Screen for Listing 10.2

10.1.3 Pie Chart

A pie chart divides up a circular region into 'slices' to show numerical proportions. Now you'll see how to create a simple pie chart using D3.

To enable you to draw a pie chart you need to be aware of two methods:

- **d3.arc()** and
- **d3.pie()** methods

The d3.arc() method
The **d3.arc()** generates an arc shape. You need to set the inner radius and the outer radius for the arc. If the inner radius is 0, the result will be a pie chart, otherwise the result will be a donut chart (which you'll learn about later).

The d3.pie() method
The **d3.pie()** method is used to generate a pie chart. It takes the data from a dataset and calculates the start angle and eng angle for each wedge of the pie chart.

Listing 10.3: Input

```
<!DOCTYPE html>
<html>
  <head>
    <script type='text/javascript' src='https://d3js.org/
        ↪ d3.v7.min.js'></script>
  </head>
  <body>

  <!-- insert the csv script file inline for testing - however,
   you can have an external url that refers to your csv data
   which is loaded in automatically by d3.csv(..) method -->
  <script id='csv' type='text/csv'>states,percentage
    Up,80.00
    Ma,70.00
    Bi,65.00
    Mp,60.00
    Gu,50.00
    Wb,49.00
    Tn,35.00
  </script>

  <script>
  let tex = document.getElementById('csv').text;
```

```
  let csv = URL.createObjectURL(new Blob([ tex ]));

  d3.csv(csv).then(function(data) {
    console.log("columns are: " + data.columns)
  })
  </script>
</body>
</html>
```

Listing 10.4: Console for Listing 10.3

```
["columns are: states,percentage"]
```

A complete pie chart example is given below:

Listing 10.5: Input

```
<!DOCTYPE html>
<html>
<head>
    <style>
        .arc text {
            font: 10px sans-serif;
            text-anchor: middle;
        }

        .arc path {
            stroke: #fff;
        }

        .title {
            fill: teal;
            font-weight: bold;
        }
    </style>
    <script src="https://d3js.org/d3.v4.min.js"></script>
</head>
<body>
    <svg width="500" height="400"></svg>

  <script id='csv' type='text/csv'>browser,percent
  Chrome,73.70
  IE/Edge,4.90
  Firefox,15.40
  Safari,3.60
  Opera,1.00
  </script>

  <script>
    let svg = d3.select("svg");
    let width = svg.attr("width");
    let height = svg.attr("height");
    let radius = Math.min(width, height) / 2;

    let g = svg.append("g")
      .attr("transform", "translate(" + width / 2 + "," + height / 2
          ↪ + ")");
```

10.1 Introduction

```
let color = d3.scaleOrdinal(['#4daf4a','#377eb8','#ff7f00','
    ↪ #984ea3','#e41a1c']);

let pie = d3.pie()
.value(function(d) {
        return d.percent;
});

let path = d3.arc()
.outerRadius(radius - 10)
.innerRadius(0);

let label = d3.arc()
.outerRadius(radius)
.innerRadius(radius - 80);

let csv = document.getElementById('csv').text;
let blob = new Blob([csv]);
let blobUrl = URL.createObjectURL(blob);

d3.csv(blobUrl, function(error, data) {
    if (error) {
        throw error;
    }
    let arc = g.selectAll(".arc")
            .data(pie(data))
            .enter().append("g")
            .attr("class", "arc");

    arc.append("path")
    .attr("d", path)
    .attr("fill", function(d) { return color(d.data.browser);
        ↪ });

    // console.log(arc)

    arc.append("text")
    .attr("transform", function(d) {
            return "translate(" + label.centroid(d) + ")";
    })
    .text(function(d) { return d.data.browser; });
});

svg.append("g")
.attr("transform", "translate(" + (width / 2 - 120) + "," +
    ↪ 20 + ")")
.append("text")
.text("Browser use statistics - Jan 2017")
.attr("class", "title")
</script>
</body>
</html>
```

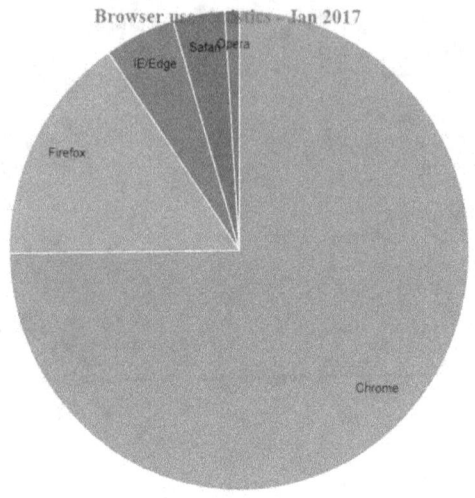

Figure 10.3: Screen for Listing 10.5

10.1.4 Donut Chart

You can modify your existing pie chart to a donut with a small modification:

```
var arc = d3.arc()
        .outerRadius(radius)
        .innerRadius(100);
```

Listing 10.6: Input

```
<!DOCTYPE html>
<html>
<head>
    <style>
        .arc text {
            font: 10px sans-serif;
            text-anchor: middle;
        }

        .arc path {
            stroke: #fff;
        }

        .title {
            fill: teal;
            font-weight: bold;
        }
```

10.1 Introduction

```
    </style>
    <script src="https://d3js.org/d3.v4.min.js"></script>
</head>
<body>
    <svg width="500" height="400"></svg>

  <script id='csv' type='text/csv'>browser,percent
  Chrome,73.70
  IE/Edge,4.90
  Firefox,15.40
  Safari,3.60
  Opera,1.00
  </script>

  <script>
    let svg = d3.select("svg");
    let width = svg.attr("width");
    let height = svg.attr("height");
    let radius = Math.min(width, height) / 2;

    let g = svg.append("g")
    .attr("transform", "translate(" + width / 2 + "," + height / 2
      ↪ + ")");

    let color = d3.scaleOrdinal(['#4daf4a','#377eb8','#ff7f00','
      ↪ #984ea3','#e41a1c']);

    let pie = d3.pie()
    .value(function(d) {
            return d.percent;
    });

    let path = d3.arc()
    .outerRadius(radius - 10)
    .innerRadius(100);

    let label = d3.arc()
    .outerRadius(radius)
    .innerRadius(radius - 80);

    let csv = document.getElementById('csv').text;
    let blob = new Blob([csv]);
    let blobUrl = URL.createObjectURL(blob);

    d3.csv(blobUrl, function(error, data) {
        if (error) {
            throw error;
        }
        let arc = g.selectAll(".arc")
              .data(pie(data))
              .enter().append("g")
              .attr("class", "arc");

        arc.append("path")
        .attr("d", path)
        .attr("fill", function(d) { return color(d.data.browser);
            ↪ });
```

```
        // console.log(arc)

        arc.append("text")
        .attr("transform", function(d) {
                    return "translate(" + label.centroid(d) + ")";
        })
        .text(function(d) { return d.data.browser; });
    });

    svg.append("g")
    .attr("transform", "translate(" + (width / 2 - 120) + "," +
        ↪ 20 + ")")
    .append("text")
    .text("Browser use statistics - Jan 2017")
    .attr("class", "title")
    </script>
</body>
</html>
```

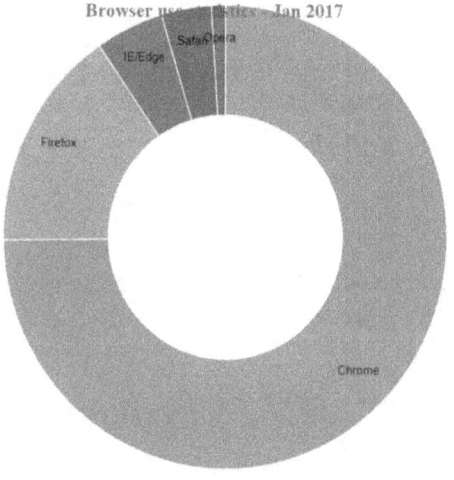

Figure 10.4: Screen for Listing 10.6

11. Examples

11.1 Variety of D3 Examples

This chapter provides a variety of examples using D3 - from simple text output to grids. Each of the examples can be typed in and run (minimalistic and self-contained). Also the output for each example listings is shown in a figure as well.

Listing 11.1: Input

```
var script = document.createElement('script');
script.src = 'https://d3js.org/d3.v4.min.js';
document.head.appendChild(script);

onload = function(){
  d3.select("body").append("span").text("Hello, world!");
}
```

Hello, world!

Figure 11.1: Screen for Listing 11.1

Listing 11.2: Input

```
var scripts = document.createElement('script');
scripts.src = 'https://d3js.org/d3.v4.min.js';
document.head.appendChild(scripts);
document.body.style.height = '60pt';

onload = function(){
  d3.select("body").append("h3").text("Hello, world!");
  d3.select('h3').style('color', 'darkblue');
  d3.select('h3').style('font-size', '24px');
}
```

Listing 11.3: Input

Hello, world!

Figure 11.2: Screen for Listing 11.2

Listing 11.4: Input

```
var scripts = document.createElement('script');
scripts.src = 'https://d3js.org/d3.v4.min.js';
document.body.appendChild(scripts);

document.body.style.height = '170px';

scripts.onload = function(){

  console.log('loaded d3js script');

  d3.select("body").selectAll("p")
   .data([10, 20, 30, 50, 70])
   .text(function(d) { return d; })
   .enter()
   .append("p")
   .text(function(d) { return d; });

  console.log('finished');
}
```

Listing 11.5: Input

```
["loaded d3js script"]
["finished"]
```

Listing 11.6: Input

```
var scripts = document.createElement('script');
scripts.src = 'https://d3js.org/d3.v4.min.js';
document.body.appendChild(scripts);
```

11.1 Variety of D3 Examples

10

20

30

50

70

Figure 11.3: Screen for Listing 11.4

```
document.body.style.height = '170px';

scripts.onload = function(){

  console.log('loaded d3js script');

var data = [ //This is the data we want to visualize.
             //In reality it usually comes from a file or
               ↪ database.
  {x: 10, y: 10},
  {x: 10, y: 20},
  {x: 10, y: 30},
  {x: 10, y: 40},
  {x: 10, y: 50},
  {x: 10, y: 80},
  {x: 10, y: 90},
  {x: 10, y: 100},
  {x: 10, y: 110},
  {x: 20, y: 30},
  {x: 20, y: 120},
  {x: 30, y: 10},
  {x: 30, y: 20},
  {x: 30, y: 30},
  {x: 30, y: 40},
  {x: 30, y: 50},
  {x: 30, y: 80},
  {x: 30, y: 90},
  {x: 30, y: 100},
  {x: 30, y: 110},
  {x: 40, y: 120},
  {x: 50, y: 10},
  {x: 50, y: 20},
  {x: 50, y: 30},
  {x: 50, y: 40},
  {x: 50, y: 50},
  {x: 50, y: 80},
  {x: 50, y: 90},
  {x: 50, y: 100},
  {x: 50, y: 110},
  {x: 60, y: 10},
```

```
{x: 60, y: 30},
{x: 60, y: 50},
{x: 70, y: 10},
{x: 70, y: 30},
{x: 70, y: 50},
{x: 70, y: 90},
{x: 70, y: 100},
{x: 70, y: 110},
{x: 80, y: 80},
{x: 80, y: 120},
{x: 90, y: 10},
{x: 90, y: 20},
{x: 90, y: 30},
{x: 90, y: 40},
{x: 90, y: 50},
{x: 90, y: 80},
{x: 90, y: 120},
{x: 100, y: 50},
{x: 100, y: 90},
{x: 100, y: 100},
{x: 100, y: 110},
{x: 110, y: 50},
{x: 120, y: 80},
{x: 120, y: 90},
{x: 120, y: 100},
{x: 120, y: 110},
{x: 120, y: 120},
{x: 130, y: 10},
{x: 130, y: 20},
{x: 130, y: 30},
{x: 130, y: 40},
{x: 130, y: 50},
{x: 130, y: 80},
{x: 130, y: 100},
{x: 140, y: 50},
{x: 140, y: 80},
{x: 140, y: 100},
{x: 140, y: 110},
{x: 150, y: 50},
{x: 150, y: 90},
{x: 150, y: 120},
{x: 170, y: 20},
{x: 170, y: 30},
{x: 170, y: 40},
{x: 170, y: 80},
{x: 170, y: 90},
{x: 170, y: 100},
{x: 170, y: 110},
{x: 170, y: 120},
{x: 180, y: 10},
{x: 180, y: 50},
{x: 180, y: 120},
{x: 190, y: 10},
{x: 190, y: 50},
{x: 190, y: 120},
{x: 200, y: 20},
{x: 200, y: 30},
{x: 200, y: 40},
```

```
  {x: 210, y: 80},
  {x: 210, y: 90},
  {x: 210, y: 100},
  {x: 210, y: 110},
  {x: 210, y: 120},
  {x: 220, y: 80},
  {x: 220, y: 120},
  {x: 230, y: 80},
  {x: 230, y: 120},
  {x: 240, y: 90},
  {x: 240, y: 100},
  {x: 240, y: 110},
  {x: 270, y: 70},
  {x: 270, y: 80},
  {x: 270, y: 90},
  {x: 270, y: 100},
  {x: 270, y: 120}
];

//The following code chains a bunch of methods. Method chaining is
    ↪ what makes d3 very simple and concise.
d3.select("body").append("svg").selectAll() //'d3' calls the d3
    ↪ library
                                    //'.select' selects the
                                        ↪ object (in this
                                        ↪ case the body of
                                        ↪ HTML)
                                    //'.append' adds SVG
                                        ↪ element to the
                                        ↪ body
                                    //'.selectAll()' selects
                                        ↪ all SVG elements
  .data(data) //'.data' gets the data from the variable 'data'
  .enter().append("circle") //'.enter' enters the data into the
        ↪ SVG
                                    //the data enter as
                                        ↪ circles with '
                                        ↪ .append("circle")
                                        ↪ '
  .attr("r", 3) //'.attr' adds/alters atributes of SVG,
                                    //such as radius ("r"),
                                        ↪ making it 3
                                        ↪ pixels
  .attr("cx", function(d) { return d.x; }) //coordinates "cx" (
        ↪ circles' x coordinates)
  .attr("cy", function(d) { return d.y; }) //coordinates "cy" (
        ↪ circles' y coordinates)
  .style("fill", "darkblue"); //'.style' changes CSS of the SVG
                                    //in this case, fills
                                        ↪ circles with "
                                        ↪ darkblue" color


  console.log('finished');
}
```

Listing 11.7: Input

```
["loaded d3js script"]
["finished"]
```

Figure 11.4: Screen for Listing 11.6

Listing 11.8: Input

```
var scripts = document.createElement('script');
scripts.src = 'https://d3js.org/d3.v4.min.js';
document.body.appendChild(scripts);

document.body.style.height = '220px';

scripts.onload = function(){

  console.log('loaded d3js script');

var svg = d3.select("body") //create Svg element
   .append("svg")
   .attr("height",200 )
   .attr("width", 200)
   .style("border", "solid 8px red");

svg.append("line")
   .attr("x1", 50)
   .attr("y1", 30)
   .attr("x2", 150)
   .attr("y2", 100)
   .attr("stroke", "black")
   .attr("stroke-width","2px");

  console.log('finished');
}
```

Listing 11.9: Input

```
["loaded d3js script"]
["finished"]
```

Listing 11.10: Input

```
var scripts = document.createElement('script');
scripts.src = 'https://d3js.org/d3.v4.min.js';
document.body.appendChild(scripts);
```

11.1 Variety of D3 Examples

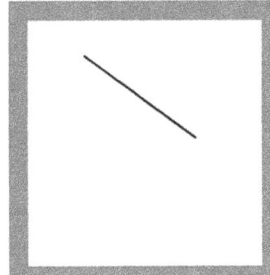

Figure 11.5: Screen for Listing 11.8

```
document.body.style.height = '220px';

scripts.onload = function(){

  console.log('loaded d3js script');

  var svg = d3.select("body") //create svg element
   .append("svg")
   .attr("height",200 )
   .attr("width", 600)
   .style("border", "solid 1px orange");

  // Create a scale: transform value in pixel
  var x = d3.scaleLinear()
      .domain([0, 100]) // This is the min and the max of the data
          ↪ : 0 to 100 if percentages
      .range([40, 300]); // This is the corresponding value I want
          ↪ in Pixel

  svg.append("g")
      .attr("transform", "translate(50, 40)")
      .call(d3.axisBottom(x));


  console.log('finished');
}
```

Listing 11.11: Input

```
["loaded d3js script"]
["finished"]
```

Listing 11.12: Input

```
var scripts = document.createElement('script');
scripts.src = 'https://d3js.org/d3.v4.min.js';
document.body.appendChild(scripts);

document.body.style.height = '420px';
```

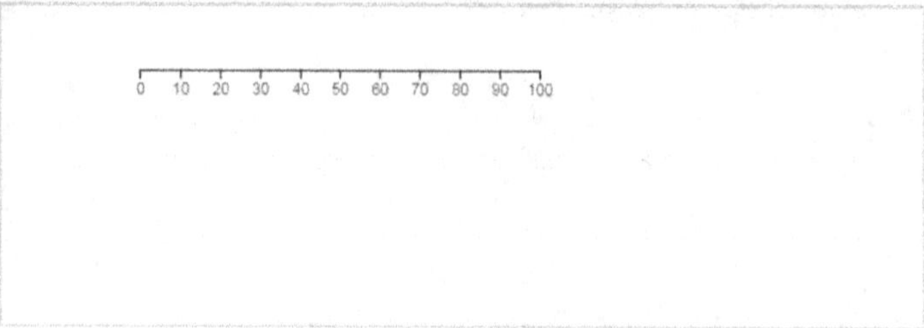

Figure 11.6: Screen for Listing 11.10

```
let scatterArea = document.createElement('div');
scatterArea.id = "scatter_area";
document.body.appendChild(scatterArea);


scripts.onload = function(){

  console.log('loaded d3js script');

// set the dimensions and margins of the graph
var margin = {top: 10, right: 40, bottom: 30, left: 30},
    width = 450 - margin.left - margin.right,
    height = 400 - margin.top - margin.bottom;

// append the svg object to the body of the page
var svG = d3.select("#scatter_area")
  .append("svg")
    .attr("width", width + margin.left + margin.right)
    .attr("height", height + margin.top + margin.bottom)
  .append("g")
    .attr("transform",
          "translate(" + margin.left + "," + margin.top + ")");

// Create data
var data = [ {x:10, y:20}, {x:40, y:90}, {x:80, y:50} ]

// X scale and Axis
var x = d3.scaleLinear()
    .domain([0, 100]) // This is the min and the max of the data:
        ↪ 0 to 100 if percentages
    .range([0, width]); // This is the corresponding value I want
        ↪ in Pixel
svG
  .append('g')
  .attr("transform", "translate(0," + height + ")")
  .call(d3.axisBottom(x));

// X scale and Axis
var y = d3.scaleLinear()
    .domain([0, 100]) // This is the min and the max of the data:
```

11.1 Variety of D3 Examples

```
        ↪ 0 to 100 if percentages
    .range([height, 0]); // This is the corresponding value I want
        ↪ in Pixel
svG
  .append('g')
  .call(d3.axisLeft(y));

// Add 3 dots for 0, 50 and 100%
svG
  .selectAll("whatever")
  .data(data)
  .enter()
  .append("circle")
    .attr("cx", function(d){ return x(d.x) })
    .attr("cy", function(d){ return y(d.y) })
    .attr("r", 7)

  console.log('finished');
}
```

Listing 11.13: Input

```
["loaded d3js script"]
["finished"]
```

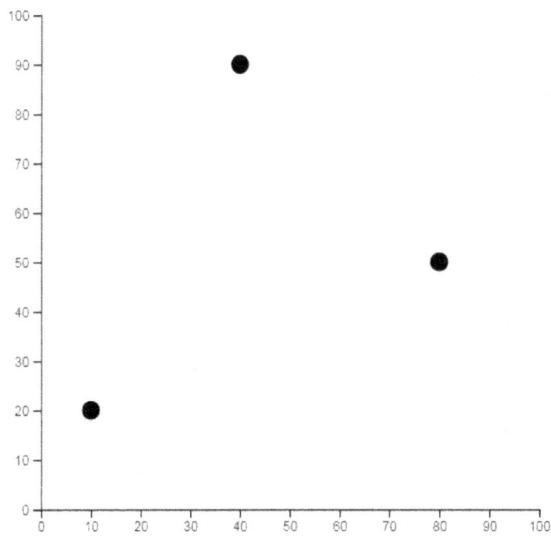

Figure 11.7: Screen for Listing 11.12

Listing 11.14: Input

```javascript
var scripts = document.createElement('script');
scripts.src = 'https://d3js.org/d3.v4.min.js';
document.body.appendChild(scripts);

document.body.style.height = '320px';

scripts.onload = function(){

  console.log('loaded d3js script');

var margin = {top: 20, right: 20, bottom: 60, left: 80},
    width = 300 - margin.left - margin.right,
    height = 300 - margin.top - margin.bottom;
var data = [
  {language: "Python", value: 30},
  {language: "Java", value: 20},
  {language: "C/C++", value: 15},
  {language: "Javascript", value: 35},
  {language: "PHP", value: 15}];
var colors=["#00A5E3","#FF96C5","#00CDAC","#FFA23A","#74737A"] ;
var svg = d3.select("body") //create Svg element
   .append("svg")
   .attr('width', width + margin.right + margin.left)
   .attr('height', height + margin.top + margin.bottom)
   .style("border", "solid 1px red")
   .attr("transform","translate(5,5)");
var chart=svg.append('g')
   .attr('transform', 'translate(' + margin.left + ',' +
       margin.top + ')')
   .attr('width', width)
   .attr('height', height)
var pie=d3.pie()
       .value(d => d.value)
var color_scale=d3.scaleOrdinal()
           .domain(data.map(d=>d.language))
           .range(colors)
let arc=d3.arc()
      .outerRadius(100)
      .innerRadius(0)
var p_chart=chart.selectAll("pie")
     .data(pie(data))
     .enter()
     .append("g")
     .attr('transform', 'translate(70,130)')
p_chart.append("path")
   .attr("d",arc)
   .attr("fill",d=>{
     return color_scale(d.data.language);
   })
p_chart.append("text")
      .text(function(d){ return d.data.language})
      .attr("transform", function(d) { return "translate(" +
          arc.centroid(d) + ")"; })
      .style("text-anchor", "middle")

  console.log('finished');
}
```

11.1 Variety of D3 Examples

Listing 11.15: Input

```
["loaded d3js script"]
["finished"]
```

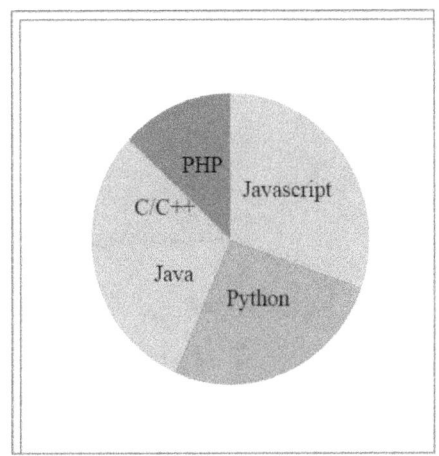

Figure 11.8: Screen for Listing 11.14

Listing 11.16: Input

```
var scripts = document.createElement('script');
scripts.src = 'https://d3js.org/d3.v4.min.js';
document.body.appendChild(scripts);

document.body.style.height = '320px';

scripts.onload = function(){

  console.log('loaded d3js script');

    var svg = d3.select("body")
        .append("svg")
        .attr("width", 500)
        .attr("height", 500);


    var bar1 = svg.append("rect")
        .attr("fill", "blue")
        .attr("x", 100)
        .attr("y", 20)
        .attr("height", 20)
        .attr("width", 10)

    var bar2 = svg.append("rect")
        .attr("fill", "blue")
        .attr("x", 120)
```

```
        .attr("y", 20)
        .attr("height", 20)
        .attr("width", 10)

    update();

function update() {
    bar1.transition()
        .ease(d3.easeLinear)
        .duration(2000)
        .attr("height",100)

    bar2.transition()
        .ease(d3.easeLinear)
        .duration(2000)
        .delay(2000)
        .attr("height",100)
}

  console.log('finished');
}
```

Listing 11.17: Input

```
["loaded d3js script"]
["finished"]
```

Listing 11.18: Input

```
var scripts = document.createElement('script');
scripts.src = 'https://d3js.org/d3.v7.min.js'; // note 'v7'
    ↪ introduces 'join' method
document.body.appendChild(scripts);

document.body.style.height = '320px';

scripts.onload = function(){

  console.log('loaded d3js script');

    var svg = d3.select("body")
        .append("svg")
        .attr("width", 500)
        .attr("height", 500);


    var data = [];

    var colors = d3.scaleOrdinal(d3.schemeSet3);

    function update(){

      var height = document.body.clientHeight;
      var width = document.body.clientWidth;
      var h = height/data.length;

      d3.select('svg')
```

11.1 Variety of D3 Examples

Figure 11.9: Screen for Listing 11.16

```
    .selectAll('rect')
    .data(data)
    .join('rect')
    .style('fill', (d, i) => colors(i))
    .transition()
    .attr('width', d => d.value * width)
    .attr('height', h-1)
    .attr('y', (d, i) => i*h)
};

function makedata(){
  var num = parseInt(Math.random()*20) + 5
  data = d3.range(num).map(d => {
    return {value:Math.random()}
  })
};

d3.select('svg').on('click', function(){
  makedata();
  update();
```

```
    });

    makedata();
    update();

    console.log('finished');
}// end onload(..)
```

Listing 11.19: Input

```
["loaded d3js script"]
["finished"]
```

Figure 11.10: Screen for Listing 11.18

Index

adding elements, 23
animations, 65
apache, 12
append, 19
append(), 23
attr(), 25, 26

bar chart, 71, 72
benefits, 4
brain, 3

cascading style sheets, 14
cdn, 7, 10
cdnjs, 10
charts, 71
chrome, 12
circle, 46
circle chart, 71, 75
class name, 20
class name selection, 21
classed(), 27
color, 65
concepts, 13
content delivery network (cdn), 10
css, 3, 14, 15

d3, 1, 2
d3 library, 8
d3-transform, 58
d3.arc(), 79
d3.js, 2

d3.pie(), 79
d3.select('svg'), 44
d3.select(..), 20, 24
d3js, 2
data functions, 38
data join, 31, 32
data-driven documents, 1
delay, 63
delay(), 67
div, 20
div.append(..), 24
document object model, 3, 14
dom, 3, 13, 14
dom elements, 23
donut chart, 71, 82
dot, 22
drawing, 71
duration(), 63, 66
dynamically, 11

ease(), 63
eclispe, 11
edge, 12
editor, 11
ellipse, 47
emcascript, 18
enter(), 37
exit(), 37

features, 4
firefox, 12
frameworks, 2

g, 54
getting started, 7
groups, 54

h1, 20
hierarchical, 13
html, 3, 14
html(), 25
humans, 3
hypertext markup language, 14

id, 20
id selection, 22
ide, 11
install, 5
installation, 7
integrated development environment, 11
interactions, 13

javascript, 1, 13, 14
join, 31, 32

license, 4
localhost, 12
loosly typed, 17

manipulation, 5
minified, 4
modify, 19
modifying elements, 25
modular, 4

notepad, 11

pie chart, 71, 79
python, 12

rect, 44, 72
rectangle, 44

remove, 19
rotate, 51
rotation, 52

scalable vector graphics, 14, 41
scale, 54, 72
schedule, 68
select(), 19
selectAll(), 19, 28
selections, 19
shapes, 13
span, 20
style(), 26
submlime text, 11
svg, 3, 14, 16, 41
svg features, 41
svg groups, 54
svg transforms, 51

tag, 20
tag identifier, 20
terms, 13
transform library, 58
transforms, 55
transition, 68
transition lifecycle, 68
transition(), 61
transitions, 61, 69
translate, 51
tweens, 70

user interfaces(ui), 13
utf8, 7

version, 4, 11
visual studio code, 11
visualization, 2

web browser, 12
web storm, 11

www.ingramcontent.com/pod-product-compliance
Lightning Source LLC
Chambersburg PA
CBHW052328220526
45472CB00001B/330